*FRITZ*

*MORE STORIES FROM*
*NEW HAMPSHIRE CHRONICLE*

# Fritz

MORE STORIES FROM NEW HAMPSHIRE CHRONICLE

*Fritz Wetherbee's*
NEW HAMPSHIRE

Fritz Wetherbee

PLAIDSWEDE PUBLISHING
Concord, New Hampshire

Copyright © 2007, by Fritz Wetherbee

All rights reserved. No part of this work may be used or reproduced in any manner whatsoever without written permission from the publisher, except in the case of brief quotations embodied in critical articles and reviews.

ISBN-13: 978-0-9790784-5-3
Library of Congress Control Number: 2007936421

Designed and composed in Minion Pro
at Hobblebush Books,
Brookline, New Hampshire (www.hobblebush.com)

Printed in the United States of America

Published by:
PLAIDSWEDE PUBLISHING
P.O. Box 269 · Concord, New Hampshire 03302-0269
www.plaidswede.com

# CONTENTS

INTRODUCTION   xi

## THE STORIES

The Fife Boy   3
The Squaw Lot   5
The Drunken Revel   6
Rainbow   8
The Country Road   10
Brotherly Love's a Honey   12
Spirits   13
Garbage to a Bear   14
Damming on the Sabbath   15
Shoplifter's Flogging   17
New Today   18
Chicken in Church   20
Indian Stream   22
Bear Fits   24
The Historic Flags   26
The Amputation   29
Toughest Winter on Record   30
Undertakers   31
The Doctor's Pay   32
Bison Man   33
Bear-Back Riding   34
The Pirate Caper   36
A Toast to a Building   38
America's First Great Trotting Horse   39
Jackson in Concord   41
The Horse Boat   43
The Great Awakening   45
Webster Comes Back to Portsmouth   46
The Bridegroom Doth Not Come   48
Manchester Log Run   49
Frost Free Library   51
The Five Trees   53
Transatlantic Cable   54

Kinky Schoolteacher   56
Dynamite Corner   57
Prices in 1895   60
Trashin'   61
Stop the Wedding!   63
Dying   65
Old Grey Bonnet   66
Lithium Spring   68
President Wilson at Harlakenden   70
Yankee Pride   72
The Klan in Charlestown   74
Cloud Seeding   76
Reserve the Right to Refuse Service   78
Lobster Dinner   79

## THE TOWNS

Barnstead   83
Benton   84
Boscawen Native   86
Bradford   87
Number Four Becomes Charlestown   88
Concord   90
Famous from Croydon   92
Francestown Soapstone   94
Garrison Hill   96
Ghost Hollow   99
Gilford   100
Goshen   101
Grafton   102
Grantham   104
Hampton Falls   105
Harrisville   106
Hebron   107
Hooksett   108
Legend of Granite Lake   109
Newington   111
Newington Meetinghouse   113
Pembroke   115
Peterborough   116

Theater in Portsmouth     117
Sharon First Vote     118
Squog     120
Swanzey Postal Rates     122
Temple     123
Usquebaugh     124
Vermont Secession     126
Warner     128

THE PEOPLE

The Acworth Wild Man     133
Isaac O. B.     135
Major Batchelder     137
The Great Bellows     139
Ben Chandler Dies on Mt. Washington     140
Governor's Calf Pasture     142
Lady Blanche     143
John Langdon's Speech     145
Lost Lead Mine     147
John Colony     148
The Grandfather Clock     150
Uncle Billy     152
Turned to Stone     153
Joe English Hill     154
John Fitch     155
Asa Fox, Murderer     157
Daniel Chester French     159
Leather French     161
Old Soldier Haines     162
Aaron's Truth and Martha's Shirts     163
Temple Glass     165
Pesky Peter     167
Jackwish     169
Lafayette in Bradford     170
Parson Leavitt     172
Lincoln Speaks     173
Long's Automobile     175
Gwin     177
Impaled on a Stake     179

Millerites    181
The Hermit of Bow Lake    182
John Morey and the Catamount    183
Murphy's Grave    184
Nancy    190
The Witch of Salem    191
Lyndeborough Silver Mine    192
Commodore Perkins    193
Over to Satan    195
The First Man to Die at Number Four    197
Priscilla Quimby's Ghost    199
The Sea Captain    201
Doctor Robb    202
Romeo and Juliet    204
Ed Shedd    205
AWOL: John Starburd    207
Molly Stark's Cannon    209
The Other John Stark    211
John Taggert's Journey    213
Snow in July    214
Richard Waldron    215
Frances Deering Wentworth    218
Martha's Second Wentworth    220
William Whipple's Wedding    222
Leonard Wood    224

THE WETHERBEES

Aunt Ethel Goosed    229
The Milkman    231
My First Horse Race    233
The Country Club    234
Fritz the Beatnik    236
Happy Birthday, Paul    238
The Candidates    240
Harold Stassen    242
Tickie Dickie    244
Gary Hart    245
Green Christmas    246
Adam Sandler    247
Thanksgiving in New Hampshire    248

## ACKNOWLEDGMENTS

I WANT TO thank the following for their support of my work and this book:

Mary Ann Mroczka, senior producer, *New Hampshire Chronicle*, WMUR-TV

Jeff Bartlett, general manager, WMUR-TV

Hearst Arguyle, for allowing me to do this book

Rick Broussard, editor of *New Hampshire Magazine*, who got this project under way

Holly Scopa, Tracey Spolter, Donna Smith, Tom Griffith and Tiffany Eddy, Chris Shepherd, Chris McDevitt, Paul Falco, Chris Orr, Ryan Murphy and the rest of the *Chronicle* gang who make my on-air job easy

George Geers and Sara Minette of Plaidswede Publishing Co.

Laura for her love, support and suggestions

— Fritz Wetherbee

INTRODUCTION

ON THE ONE-YEAR anniversary of "New Hampshire Chronicle," Fritz Wetherbee ate crow.

We tend to define the people we see on television according to our own experience. It's only natural. After all, these folks invite themselves into our homes each night. So Fritz Wetherbee has come to be a lot of different things to a lot of people. To some, he's a master storyteller, author, and historian . . . a moniker which makes him wince. To others, the guy with the bowtie and the voice is the beloved grandfather they never had. Many have asked if we would fix him up with mother. As the most popular celebrity in the state . . . ask him about the time he was mobbed in a Wal-Mart . . . he could easily swing the New Hampshire Primary one way or the other should he be inclined to put his name on the ballot. President Wetherbee. Has a nice ring to it.

But to me, he is first and foremost a teacher.

My education began back in the mid 1980s, when we worked together many late nights producing segments at New Hampshire Public Television. I would labor over a script, choosing just the right words then run it by the master hoping for his approval. Kindly, but firmly, he would remind me that writing for broadcast is a different beast than writing a term paper. The language must be conversational. "People don't talk that way! Write as if you're talking with a friend. Words must never be longer than three syllables. No more than seventeen words in a sentence!"

Indeed, his conversational style has come to educate an entire state.

Fritz has trained television audiences to do something unheard of in this day and age. Simply sit and listen. There are no flashy graphics or fancy editing when he "tells us a story." No need to distract or bedazzle. He speaks directly to us about things we didn't even realize we cared about, until he lends it his "street cred." Do you know how the town of Hebron got its name? Cockermouth didn't stick. Or that William Whipple, one of the three New Hampshire men to sign the Declaration of Independence, was left at the altar? Still, the tales that resonate the most are his personal reminiscences. You smell the smoky coffeehouses during the days when Fritz was "a serious Beatnik". You taste the fried chicken and beer he ate with honor as the only white guest in a segregated "country club." And you cheer our hero on each year when he takes on Adam Sandler for the tongue-in-cheek title of New Hampshire's biggest star in the "Best of New Hampshire" poll. As a writer for broadcast, no one can compare. It's as if his stories aren't written at all. They are impromptu recollections told off the top of his head. Friend to friend.

That being said, Fritz does not forsake the visual power of our medium. He is also a master of our visual language, having been a cinematographer at one point in his career. Our team of videographers was accustomed to shooting stories for newscasts before working on "New Hampshire Chronicle." They are often required to work at a fast, "get the job done and get out of there" pace. Collaborating with Fritz became an eye-opening experience for many of them. "Tighter... wider... lower angles... slower moves... the use of perspective... let's try it this way." Their creative juices began to flow, and shooting with Fritz soon became the highlight of the week. The crew cherishes their "Fritz Fridays," when cameraman, producer, and talent collaborate to push the envelope, working to tell the tale the way it needs to be told.

So how did this master teacher end up eating a tasty plate of fresh crow? I don't mean to imply that Fritz is a "glass is half empty" kind of guy, but he is humble to the end and has a tendency to underestimate himself. We were merely asking him to do the impossible. Give us five unique stories about New Hampshire every week. Research them, write them, then shoot them all in one day with little to no post-production time. A cinch, right? Fritz thought his well of good stories would run dry fairly quickly. Five a week! Are they nuts? People wouldn't watch. It couldn't be done. Well, he was partially right, it couldn't be done . . . by anyone else.

So, on the first anniversary of "New Hampshire Chronicle," Fritz sat down and told the story of his own nay-saying. The camera started tight and slowly revealed him holding a knife and fork, seated in front of a plate overflowing with a stuffed, metaphorical crow. That was well over 1,000 stories ago. Darned if it wasn't delicious.

Maryann M. Mroczka
*Executive Producer*
*New Hampshire Chronicle*
*WMUR-TV*
*July 2007*

# THE STORIES

## The Fife Boy

TWO PAINTINGS OF the American Revolution are firmly etched in the consciousness of patriotic America.

The first is the Emanuel Gottlieb Leutze picture, *Washington Crossing the Delaware,* and the other is that Archibald Willard picture titled *The Spirit of '76*, which pictures three men emerging from the smoke of battle playing music. There are two drummers, a young boy and an old man . . . and on their left marches a man with a bandaged head playing the fife.

Over the course of my life I have seen this tableau repeated in the movies and in parades. And it came to mind the other day while reading the history of Goshen, New Hampshire.

It seems that, in the re-enactments of this trio, the two drummers and the fife player, the fife player with the bandage always marches with a limp. He is the one of soldierly age and has clearly been in the thick of it. He is wounded.

Now for the story.

Seems back in 1774, a man named Captain Murray visited the Fort at Number Four in Charlestown, and there he met a young man from the town of Goshen, New Hampshire.

The young man was Oliver Corey Jr. and he played the fife. He played so well, in fact, that Captain Murray was impressed.

Later, right after the Battle of Bunker Hill, Captain Murray wrote a letter to Oliver Corey's father. In it he asked if the young man could come down to Cambridge and be the fifer for Colonel Woodbridge's regiment.

Seems that the regiment's current fifer was a man named Adams and he had one leg that was shorter than the other and Colonel Woodbridge was determined to get rid of him because he thought the man's awkward gate made a bad appearance.

And it is this that brought to mind the *Spirit of '76* painting.

You gotta remember, these were different times and people were crueler.

Anyhow, the upshot was that, two days later, Oliver Corey Jr. arrived in Cambridge.

He was told that he would first have to serve as a private until they found a way to fire the present fifer.

And so for just five days Oliver soldiered. During this time, he was a sentinel guarding the house where General Washington himself was billeted. He then became the fifer for a year for Colonel Sergeant's regiment. That autumn he was sent to New York.

He marched with General Sullivan's troops at Trenton that Christmas night, and at Morristown he stood beside General Washington himself as he urged his men to re-enlist and to stay with him. He saw that day on the cheek of the great general a single tear trickle down and, with most of the rest of the troops, he, too, re-volunteered for another six weeks.

Now there are two amazing things about this story.

The first is that during his entire enlistment, Oliver Corey Jr. never once left his post. He served continuously the entire war. He was never absent a single day and never took even a single furlough.

And the second amazing thing about this story is that, when he volunteered and arrived in Cambridge . . . Oliver Corey Jr. was only eleven years old.

# The Squaw Lot

THE STORY GOES that way back in 1726, a beautiful woman of the Penacook tribe was kidnapped from her husband by Chief Peorawarrah, who came by canoe up the Merrimack River from a village south of what is now Nashua.

The kidnapper and his victim spent their first night on Sewall's Island in the northern part of what is now Concord.

The next morning, as the couple started from the island in a canoe, a shot rang out.

Ebeneezer Virgin, one of the original Concord settlers, was in the vicinity with his sons, and they heard the shot and came running.

There in the river they saw the canoe empty and the two bodies floating away down the river. Apparently the errant couple had been shot to death by the woman's husband.

Ebaneezer Virgin waded into the river and retrieved Chief Peorawarrah's rifle which he saw lying on the bottom of the river. For many years the rifle was passed on to generations in the Virgin family and the story told over and over.

Chief Peorawarrah's body was never recovered, but the woman's body washed ashore in east Concord where it was buried near the water.

And to this day, the place where the body washed ashore is called "The Squaw Lot."

# The Drunken Revel

OUT ON WHAT is now Mountain Road in east Concord, back in 1732, there sat a wigwam of a Penacook chief, Chief Pehaungun. He was, legend has it, the last of the Penacook tribe.

The Penacook Indians were the tribe that fought the first settlers in Concord.

There were thousands of Native Americans in the area when Captain John Smith first saw the Isles of Shoals, but by 1732 only about half had survived. It was not the European settlers' guns that decimated the Native American tribes, but rather smallpox and typhus and measles and other diseases that were brought here.

The land where the chief had his hogan was owned, or at least claimed, by Captain Ebeneezer Eastman, and one night the good captain heard a great ruckus coming from the chief's home.

The captain went into the hogan to find the chief and a half-dozen other male Native Americans dead drunk and literally whooping it up. Chief Pehaungun was delighted to see Captain Eastman and insisted that he have a drink. The men were drinking rum directly from the bung hole of a keg. Captain Eastman picked up the keg and put it to his lips but let most of the liquor run onto the ground.

The chief was incensed and drew a knife. He was going to kill the captain. But Captain Eastman laughed good-naturedly and made a hasty retreat from the hogan.

The next morning the captain visited the hogan again. Inside were all the Native American men sleeping it off . . . all except Chief Pehaungun. The chief lay on his animal robes in the middle of his hogan. He was dead.

The other Indians awoke and were very afraid. They feared that because the chief had threatened death to the captain, the Great Spirit was angry and had killed him. They also were afraid that the chief's spirit was still there and would haunt them.

So they buried him in a hollow log which they covered over with a slab of pine and bound with rushes from the river. They buried him deep and danced on the clay as it covered the casket, tamping it down, as it were, so that the chief's spirit could not get out to haunt them.

Afterwards, they traced the shape of the grave of Chief Pehaungun with willow branches which they stuck in the ground.

And when that was done, the history tells us, they drank the rest of the rum.

# Rainbow

BETWEEN 1740 AND 1755, the settlers on the Connecticut River suffered from hundreds of attacks by Native Americans.

This was the time of the French and Indian Wars. Around the forts all up and down the river, there wasn't a family that had not lost someone to ambush or massacre.

Fort Dummer, the "Fort at Number Three" in Walpole, the "Fort at Number Four" in Charlestown, Bridgeman's Fort and Shattuck's Fort all had attacks and terrible fighting.

The area was poorly defended. Both New Hampshire and Massachusetts were slow in sending reinforcements or supplies.

The enemy, that is the French, did not know how poorly supplied these places were.

In 1747, the blockhouse at Fort Bridgeman was burned to the ground by a contingent of thirty-five French and Indians.

Across the river facing each other, Fort Dummer and Fort Hinsdale were preparing for the siege they knew was on the way.

This same year, a Captain Alexander was reconnoitering in the area around Fort Hinsdale when he suddenly confronted a young French officer who seemed to have gotten separated from his unit.

Captain Alexander aimed his musket and the French officer fell.

He left him for dead in the forest and returned to his unit in Northfield.

Four days later, the same French soldier gave himself up at the fort in Northfield wounded, dirty, hungry and lost . . . but not dead. The surgeon at the fort bound the man's wounds and in a week or two he was healthy again.

The French officer turned out to be a young cadet named Pierre Raimbaut. He was handsome and bright and friendly, and the men at the fort took a liking to him.

Because of his last name, Raimbaut, the men nicknamed him "Rainbow."

Whether Captain Alexander had a guilty conscience about trying to kill the man or maybe he just liked him, whatever it was, the prisoner was not confined to quarters but was allowed to roam at will around the fort and the area.

Down at Fort Hinsdale, Colonel Ebenezer Hinsdale was livid. "Rainbow" was due for prisoner exchange with the French in a few weeks and he had seen way too much. He knew how thinly manned the forts were. He knew where everything was and where everyone lived.

"Nonsense," Captain Alexander said, "the man is a gentleman and he likes us."

Of course, Colonel Hinsdale was right. That very summer Rainbow was back with a contingent of troops and Indians, and they ambushed Sgt. Thomas Taylor and sixteen men just outside Fort Hinsdale. Four men were killed and eight were captured and taken to Canada for ransom.

For years Rainbow continued to harass the troops on the frontier.

And to his last breath, Colonel Hinsdale cursed Captain Alexander.

# *The Country Road*

JOHN DENVER WROTE the song "Take Me Home Country Road" back in 1973. But the original "Country Road" is a lot older than that; two hundred years older, in fact.

That road, which was actually called the "Country Road," ran from Portsmouth to Newburyport, and it was one of the most important thoroughfares in Colonial America.

It was over Country Road that the first stagecoach in America ran its regular passenger and mail route beginning in April of 1761.

It was up Country Road that Paul Revere raced in December of 1774 to inform John Langdon and the Committee of Safety that the British had ordered no military stores or arms would henceforth be imported into the Colonies.

It was this news that forced Major Langdon and John Sullivan to attack Fort William and Mary in Newcastle and make off with all the guns and ammunition stored there. These were the guns and ammunition used at Bunker Hill.

And that Paul Revere ride was five months earlier than the one to Concord and Lexington.

George Washington rode over Country Road up from Newburyport in October of 1789 on his visit to Portsmouth.

The Marquis de Lafayette also took this route on his visit in June of 1871.

General Winfield Scott came up the Country Road in 1839 on his way to Maine to settle the Aroostok War. This was a boundary dispute between the United States and New Brunswick. The Treaty of 1842 settled that matter.

It took a day and a half to go from Portsmouth to Boston in the early days.

The Country Road was the mail route. At first the mail was carried by horseback and later by stagecoach. The earlier horseback method was before the road was improved and a round trip took five days ... Portsmouth to Boston and back. Later it took only eight hours to get to Boston on the express stage. Cost, three dollars.

Today, the Country Road is gone; replaced over time by other highways: the Boston Post Road, Exeter Road, and a hundred other thoroughfares.

And a note here, most people think that Lafayette Road (Route One) in Portsmouth is called so because this was the part of the Country Road that the Marquis de Lafayette traveled on his way up from Newburyport.

Alas, Lafayette Road was named for the general but it hadn't been built when he visited there. ⁃

# Brotherly Love's a Honey

THIS STORY COMES from the Dublin town history, and it is reputed to be true. It is also a parable, that is, it has a moral meaning to go with the narrative.

Seems among the earliest settlers in the area then designated School District Number Three was a family by the name of Russell. There were two sons in the family, John and Simon, and they were hellions. They were in their early twenties when this story took place.

Now these two young men were unmarried and generally made trouble wherever they went. They caroused and drank and were forever getting into fistfights.

One day one of the brothers, and we don't know which, but one of the brothers discovered a swarm of wild bees in a hollow tree in the woods and, because he discovered it, he laid claim to it. By the end of the summer, it would be full of honey.

Unfortunately the hollow tree and the hive were located on land that belonged to the other brother, and he said, nothing doing, as it is on my land, this is my hive.

Well, toward the end of the season the brother who had discovered the tree snuck back with an ax and began chopping it down.

But the second brother heard the chopping and arrived just as his brother was setting a fire made of leaves at the end of the fallen tree to smoke the bees out and get the honey.

He at once fell upon his sibling and the two commenced to thrash each other. There were bloody noses and scratched faces until one of them hollered, "Uncle."

They then went to the tree only to find that the fire had done too good a job and had not only smoked out the bees, but had burned up the entire hive, honey and all.

"Such is the result," the town history tells us, "of many a quarrel."

## *Spirits*

IN COLONIAL TIMES there were inns in every town and city in the country. And every inn also had a place to imbibe spirits. The surprise is how much these tavern spirits were like what we drink today.

The whiskeys and rums and gins were usually displayed in glass decanters with glass stoppers on a shelf behind the bar. Like today, it was an enticement.

According to the Lebanon town history, a wine glass filled with spirits cost "four pence, ha' penny" and a gill (which is about a quarter pint) was nine pence. When the booze was mixed with sugar and water it was called a "sling" and cost the same.

A popular libation was a glass of gin with sugar and water, a dash of Stoughton's bitters, and ground nutmeg, served with a toasted cracker jammed on the rim so it stuck up in the air. This was called (are you ready for this?) a "cocktail."

People, it seems, drank all the time back then. There was even a morning toddy to get people going for the day. Kinda like orange juice today.

A "Flip" was the favorite drink in the taverns in wintertime. A Flip started with a half-pint of beer sweetened with brown sugar and heated with a "loggerhead" which was an iron rod with a thick, heavy head kept red-hot in the coals of the fire. After heating the beer, the bartender added a glass of Santa Cruz rum and a glass of brandy, the white of an egg, and he finished it with a sprinkle of nutmeg. The Flip would froth and cover a man's mustache and clean out his sinuses.

There is an old story worth telling here. It is about a Dutch judge who confronted a man brought before him for drunkenness.

"What did you get drunk on?" the judge asked.

"On punch, Your Honor."

"Then I will not fine you for I get drunk on punch myself, sometimes."

And so it was ... back then.

# Garbage to a Bear

JOSEPH MOSES WAS a memorable character in Portsmouth.

He had been born in England but he came to the city in the mid-eighteenth century to work as a house carpenter. He built a home on the corner of Fleet and Congress streets and lived there with his family for fifty years.

Moses was known as a wit and a practical joker. He once sent a man into the city council rooms, telling him it was a place he could purchase nails. The man entered and asked for a pound of single tens.

The councilors were insulted but soon learned that Moses had been at the root of it all. They summoned him and made him kneel and ask forgiveness. That he did, but on rising, he looked at his knees and brushed them off intoning, "A dirty house, a dirty house." The councilors understood the double-entendre but could do nothing about it.

Moses accompanied the Hon. Theodore Atkinson to a Congressional Delegation meeting in 1754. Moses had come along as a companion and gofer and also because he amused the Honorable Atkinson.

The story goes that one night Atkinson and other delegates were at the punch bowl discussing matters, and Joseph Moses was also at the punch bowl, and after a few more drinks than he should have had, he said to the Honorable Mr. Atkinson, "You ain't fit to carry garbage to a bear!"

The Honorable Mr. Atkinson was livid. "Man," he said, "you are too bold. I cannot receive such a remark from you. You must either recall your words or quit my service!"

"Well, I'll take them back," said Joseph Moses. "You are fit."

And nothing more was ever said on the subject.

# *Damming on the Sabbath*

BACK IN COLONIAL times, the Second Commandment was very important ... resting on the seventh day and worshipping the Lord.

About the middle of the eighteenth century, the French family started to construct a new dam on the Skowhegan River just upstream from what is now French Village. A dam meant power for sawing lumber and grinding wheat.

Dams back then were made of heavy timbers, which were laid on the bed of the river. Here they were pegged together and, when ready, tipped up much as a wall of a building.

Of course the timbers were much heavier than a house wall; so heavy, in fact, that it was not uncommon for fifty men to be required to lift it ... virtually the entire adult male population of a town like Wilton.

Well, the wall for the dam was built by Saturday and ready to be lifted in place on Monday. But it rained all day Saturday, and Sunday morning it was pouring. It appeared that an entire month's work would be washed away if the dam was not lifted before the floodwaters came.

And so, only as many men as would be required to lift that wall stayed away from church that Sunday.

The Wilton town history has the story as related by Ephram Brown later in his life. Here is what he is quoted as saying:

> The men are at the dam site. At a command they lift the heavy beams from the ground each man exerting his utmost strength.
>
> Slowly the massive timbers are carried up to the breasts of the men. But here they ceased to move higher. Again and again did these men struggle and strain but no effort could carry the timbers any higher. But neither could they let them back down. To do so was to be crushed.
>
> They were in a trap. There could be no relief except re-enforcement. But the people were at the town's center, worshipping God. But there was no man that could be spared to run to the church.

So they hollered. At a given command every man with his utmost voice shouted 'Help! Come!' and 'Help! Come!' again and again. To this day they do not know how this call for help was heard way up in the Center. It is a full mile and a half away. But it was heard and the congregation burst from the church on a run.

Fifteen minutes is the fastest any person could run the distance from the church to the dam site.

Meanwhile the men there were holding on, but their strength was failing. As they strove, the daughter of James French mixed a potion of strong drink and went from man to man pouring the rum into their mouths. The town history tells us that this enabled the men to hold out. For hold out they did and soon other arms were lifting along with them and the dam was raised in one great cheer.

It is not said whether or not the men then went back to church to give thanks, but they did finish the rum.

## Shoplifter's Flogging

SHOPLIFTING IS NOT new. Certain people have always given in to light finger work if they thought they could get away with it. The difference is that the punishment for stealing used to be a good deal more severe. A case in point:

On a cold day in January back in 1764, a woman entered a small shop on the corner of Congress and Fleet streets in Portsmouth. The Franklin block sits there today. Inside she was seen secreting a pair of children's shoes beneath her hooded cape.

When the woman left the shop, the salesperson told the owner about the missing shoes and the owner rushed outside and began yelling, "Stop, thief!"

The woman ran, but not far. A man named Goodman Newmarch rushed from his home across the street and soon caught the lady. Sure enough, she had the stolen shoes on her person.

They then bodily carried the woman to the house of the Honorable Hunking Wentworth, justice of the peace, just west of the Old North Church.

The evidence was produced and the justice heard testimony and he issued his verdict. The woman was to be publicly whipped.

She was carried to Market Square where the whipping post was the town pump. Here her hands were tied to staples on the sides of the wooden pump. Her shoulders and back were bared and the sheriff applied ten lashes.

The newspaper reported the story like this:

"Last Friday one of our female pilferers received flagellation at the whipping post, where a great number of spectators saw this good work performed; and it is hoped that others, who so justly deserve it, will soon be brought to the same place to receive their desserts."

Pretty severe, I'd say. I mean, this was all to get shoes for the baby, after all.

# New Today

BACK BEFORE THE Revolution, Rock Street in Portsmouth was as far as the city went. After that, there was a meadow and a ropewalk, which extended as far up to what is now Cornwall Street.

In case you don't know (as I didn't), a ropewalk is an area used for weaving rope. Great lengths of rope required a long walk to weave the fibers. Portsmouth was a major sailing port back then, and rope making was a profitable business.

That's all that there was out there: a meadow and a long, straight path where strands of fiber were hauled by oxen and on the shoulders of workmen as the twisting was done at one end.

The meadow was called Rock Meadow (which is where Rock Street gets its name) and at the top of the hill there was a huge boulder. From the top of that boulder it was possible to see the entire city of Portsmouth and the Navy Yard and Agamenticus Mountain way across the Piscataqua River.

It was pretty romantic. Local kids played there. Another attraction just up the way was called "the old cellar," and the old cellar was the subject of great speculation.

It was an old cellar hole that had filled with water; a place to catch frogs in the summer and to skate in the winter. The young boys loved going there.

Here's the story of how the old cellar came to be.

Seems there was an Englishman named Myrick who became enamored with Portsmouth and purchased a number of acres in the western part of the Rock Meadow. He then had plans drawn up for a fine house and a beautiful park to be built around the house.

He had the cellar hole dug and announced he was returning to England to get money and decoration for his dream. The problem was that it was a time when we were not friendly with England, and he could not book passage from Portsmouth or Boston. What he could do was sail to Jamaica and there pick up a ship to England. And so he boarded a ship in Portsmouth bound for Jamaica.

And Mr. Myrick was never heard from again.

Now, there is a story about one of the men who worked on the ropewalk, a man named George Boyde.

Seems George Boyde just up and quit his job one day to the surprise and consternation of his friends. He just threw his rope on the ground and proclaimed that he would never spin another thread. "I'll get my living in an easier way," he said.

And so he did. Somehow he got hold of some capital and went into business and died a wealthy man.

No one ever knew where he got his seed money, but the speculation was that he had found Mr. Myrick's hidden stash near the old cellar. Most speculated that Myrick had been lost at sea, but to this day no one knows for sure.

No one claimed Mr. Myrick's land, by the way, and it reverted back to the original proprietors.

# Chicken in Church

THE LEBANON MEETINGHOUSE, years ago, was like most of the churches in New England. There was the main part of the church with the pews divided by partitions, there was a balcony and the pulpit.

The pulpit was about ten feet above the floor, about the height of a basketball hoop. A very steep stairway (almost a ladder) led to the pulpit.

Directly beneath the pulpit was the deacon's seat. And directly above the pulpit was the sounding board.

Now the sounding board was a heavy disc with a cone-shaped top, sort of like the roof of a gazebo that hung by a chain over the place where the minister spoke. The reason for the sounding board was to amplify the voice of the speaker.

And it worked. The minister's voice would reflect off the bottom of the sounding board and would allow him to be heard all over the sanctuary.

Little girls and boys would sometimes fantasize about the heavy sounding board suddenly letting go and crushing the preacher during a particularly dull and long sermon (and, I guess, some not-so-young people would do likewise). But there is no recorded story of any sounding board crushing anyone.

There is a funny story about the sounding board of the meetinghouse in Lebanon.

Seems that back in the eighteenth century the local minister was telling his flock about sin when he suddenly had competition from someone (or something) in the balcony.

"Cluck, cluck," said the voice.

The Reverend looked up to see a hen on the balcony railing competing with him for the center of attention and clearly winning.

No one knew how the hen happened to get into the church that Sunday but, nevertheless, there she was.

"Cluck, cluck," she said.

"This is outrageous!" the Reverend replied. "Do something!"

The Tithing man was on his feet. As he approached the hen, she flew off the balcony and on to the top of the sounding board. And there she sat for the rest of the service.

She, having the highest perch in the building and clearly the center of attention, settled down and made no more noise save for joining in when the hymns were sung.

No one bothered her as no one could, and, after the service when she was alone, she flew down of her own accord.

And the story would have been forgotten save for the fact that the hen left what the history calls "autograph scratches" in the top of the sounding board which were visible from the gallery for many years thereafter.

# Indian Stream

WHAT DO YOU think of this? North of West Stewartstown there is a small rivulet that runs back and forth over the border between Canada, New Hampshire and Vermont.

It is called "Hall's Stream," and there is a story about how it got its name. And, by the way, did you ever notice that little projection of Vermont that cuts into New Hampshire there? It is the only place in New Hampshire where you may travel southwest into Vermont. I'll tell you abut that after I tell you about Hall's Stream.

The story goes that after the American army invaded Canada in 1776, the troops were in disarray. General Montgomery failed in his attempt to capture Quebec, and morale was low. Many of his men deserted. Among them was a soldier named Hall.

Hall had walked away from the battle and was walking south through the woods trying to get back home. He had not eaten in days, and when he came to the stream he lay down to drink but was too weak to rise up again.

When they found him days later, the water was still rippling through his long hair. And from that time on the rivulet has been called Hall's Stream.

Now as to the strange lump in the map at the border between Vermont, Canada and New Hampshire. See, on a map, if you follow the border up the Connecticut River, right there north of Stewartstown you have a choice of rivers. The border follows generally the direction of Hall's Stream . . . but if, instead, you took the eastern stream, the one called Indian Stream, then there is no little jut on the map.

And that's kinda what happened. In the early days they didn't know where the border between Canada and New Hampshire was. The township of what is now Pittsburg had settlers from both the United States and Canada living there. Those from Canada wanted Canada to govern them. Those from the United States wanted to be in New Hampshire.

There was a real feud (not to say a war) going on there. It was such a mess that in 1829 the people living there said, in effect, "a pox on both your houses," and they set up their own country.

I'm not kidding.

In 1829, there was Canada and the United States and "The United Inhabitants of the Indian Stream Territory." They elected a Supreme Council of five people to govern them. They established a judiciary. From the standpoint of the number of people, it was the smallest independent democratic country ever formed, and it lasted five years.

But in 1842 the country was dissolved with the signing of the Ashburton Treaty between the United States and Great Britain (remember, Canada was part of Great Britain then). This treaty gave the territory to New Hampshire.

But the Indian Stream, you'll note on a map, veers off eastward before we get to the northernmost border of Vermont and that veer-off is problematic.

They solved it with that little lump of land which follows, sort of, the Indian Stream.

Here's what I think. I think we ought to take over that silly little lump of land and declare our own country. We'll call it Lump.

# Bear Fits

BACK IN 1777, one Eleazer Wilcox was troubled with bears getting at his hogs.

Mr. Wilcox lived with his family on a farm in Gilsum over near the Keene border.

One morning in early June he came out of his house to find a large bear staring him in the face. This was the culprit that was killing his pigs.

Back in he went and took out his long musket, and when I say, "long," I mean the weapon was a full five feet.

The weapon was already loaded and Eleazer got off a shot. But the bear was merely wounded and lumbered off into the woods.

So Eleazer sent one of his kids to summon his friend, Joshua Osgood, over in Sullivan. And, sure enough, Josh came with his weapon, and the two men took a dog and went in search of the wounded beast.

The two hunters took parallel tracks through the woods. They could hear each other but were not within sight of one another.

The dog suddenly became excited, and then, only about six feet in front of him, the wounded bear suddenly stood up from behind a fallen log and, with a ferocious growl, lunged at Eleazer.

He, for his part, pointed the long musket and pulled the trigger.

It was a flash in the pan. That is to say, the flint ignited the powder in the flash pan but it did not set the charge off in the barrel. It misfired!

The bear reached out and swatted the gun so hard that it bent the barrel and put a large gash in the stock.

It then leaped on Eleazer with its paws on his shoulders and began ripping at his body.

Eleazer was hollering for his friend, Josh, to come quick and the dog was biting the bear's legs.

Josh arrived as the bear was bending Eleazer backwards and to the ground.

Eleazer got hold of the bear's tongue and was pulling it out of his mouth so the beast could not bite but the bear was tearing at him with her claws.

The beast and the man were so entwined that Josh could not get off a clear shot, but one thing was certain, and that was that his friend was going to die if he did not shoot and maybe a death by gunshot was better.

So he shot.

He missed his friend and got the bear, but, again, the bear was only wounded and lumbered off into the woods.

Josh examined his friend. There was blood everywhere. Much of Eleazor's body was torn to bits. He did not think his friend would live.

Later, in fact, they counted forty-two deep lacerations.

Josh then ran to town to get help. A dozen men arrived and made a litter from spruce boughs and carried him home.

It appeared hopeless but, day by day, Eleazer got better and soon was able to walk and work. He had severe back trouble and there were days when he was in extreme pain due to the weather or overexertion.

On these days his family said he was having "bear fits," and he had them his whole life.

And the bear? The bear was found the day after the battle down beside the Ashuelot River where she had finally succumbed to her wounds.

# The Historic Flags

*The Tuck Library sits on Park Street, across the street from the State House.*

THE TUCK LIBRARY is the original building of the New Hampshire Historical Society in Concord.

Inside are most of the paper artifacts of the society and quite a few paintings and other historical objects.

However, most of the displays nowadays are in the big building in Eagle Square just off Main Street, across from the Capitol building.

But the gorgeous building on Park Street is still the symbol of the society.

Inside you will find a rotunda and a stairway leading to a landing. Look to your left and to your right and you will see, on the walls, two ancient flags.

These are among the most important artifacts the society owns. For these flags are the only American battle flags ever captured in the Revolutionary War.

Oh, there are banners from the Civil War. Thousands of banners, in fact, survive from the Civil War.

But you are looking at two of the very few flags to survive the Revolution, and the only flags of the American side ever to be captured.

These banners were carried by the New Hampshire Second Regiment. They'd been paid for and presented to the regiment by the Committee of Safety in Exeter a couple years before—cost, about thirty pounds.

How did these artifacts survive? And how were they captured in the first place?

Well, how they survived is easy. For over a hundred years they hung on the wall of an English estate where the temperature and humidity were, for some reason, about perfect.

But how they were captured, or where, are questions difficult to answer.

The original story, passed down in the family of the English colonel who took them back to Britain, was that they were part of the spoils in a battle that took place at Fort Anne, New York, in 1777.

This fight took place after our troops, the Colonial troops, had abandoned Fort Ticonderoga.

Ticonderoga, you may know, was where the first great American victory of the war occurred when Benedict Arnold and Ethan Allen defeated General John Burgoyne and the Brits.

The Americans occupied the fort for a year.

But Burgoyne showed up again and . . . well, managed to pull a couple cannons to the top of Bread Loaf Hill behind the fort.

The Americans had thought it impossible to get cannon up such a steep place and had failed to reinforce the hill.

So, on the Fourth of July, Colonial General Arthur Sinclair looked out to see the artillery pointing directly at him . . . and he ordered the fort abandoned. The troops snuck out during the night.

The Americans were skedadeling, and the Brits, in the form of the Scottish Ninth Regiment of Foot, were trailing them.

At Fort Anne—this is a few miles east of the southern part of Lake George—the troops stood and resisted. The American troops were good and would have won the battle had their ammunition not run out and had the Brits not been reinforced.

It was at this battle, according to the Fort Anne Historical Society, that the Brits captured the first American flag that had thirteen stripes . . . that is, the first American flag as we now know it. That flag has disappeared but it was described at the time in a diary.

It was at Fort Anne, the original story goes, that the Brits also captured the New Hampshire Second Regiment banners.

Good story... except later on scholars determined that the Second New Hampshire flag was not at Fort Anne.

Today many historians believe that these banners were part of what the Ninth Regiment of Foot found at Fort Ticonderoga after it was abandoned.

Either way, the commander of the Ninth, Colonel Hill, took the banners back to England with him. There they hung in the family's great hall until 1912 when Edward Tuck, one of the founders of the Historical Society and the man for whom the building is named, purchased them and gave them to the society.

You'll note that one of the banners, the blue one, is clearly the New Hampshire Second's Guidon. Its name is on it.

But the second flag, the buff one (and an aside here: preservationists think this flag was originally white) has the same symbols that the Colonial currency had: the motto "We Are One" with rings representing the thirteen original states.

This may have been one of the original national flags of our nation... or it may have represented something else. They just don't know.

It is worth a visit to this hallowed hall to see these banners and to contemplate.

# The Amputation

BACK JUST AFTER the American Revolution, a guy named Richard Potter was cutting logs out of the forest about four miles from his home in Loudon.

His team of oxen was pulling an especially large log across a hillside when it suddenly slid sideways and caught his leg between it and a smaller tree.

Mr. Potter could not move. His leg was crushed. He called out for help but it was hours before anyone found him.

He was carried home, but he was, by this time, ashen grey. Three doctors came and all concluded that amputation was useless, that Mr. Potter was a goner. It was only a matter of hours before he would be dead.

But after two of the doctors left, Dr. Carrigan thought it would be worth the attempt of amputating the leg, and he and a neighbor, Ben Thompson, tied the patient to the bed, gave him a bottle of rum, and commenced the operation.

First, according to the Concord history, he cut the flesh around the bone just below the knee. He then took from his bag a saw and commenced sawing. But the saw was very dull and it was long and tedious work. By this time the patient had passed out and was feeling nothing.

Ben told the doctor that he had a sharper saw at home and he went on the run to fetch it. Sure enough, it was a good deal sharper and the doctor finished the operation.

To hasten healing, the doctor heated rum and poured it over the bare bone. He then roughened the end of the bone with an awl.

Next night the patient was sentient and talking.

Within a couple months, Richard Potter had recovered and had fashioned for himself an artificial leg out of wood with which he not only could walk but could actually run and wrestle.

He lived in good health until July 6, 1828, when he died in bed at the age of eighty-four.

# Toughest Winter on Record

WHAT WAS THE toughest winter on record in the United States?

That's easy: the winter of 1779 to 1780.

A lot of men that year were away from their farms, gone to heed the call from Lexington and Concord. Some left their plows in the furrows of their fields and did not get back for six or seven years.

There was inflation. "Not worth a Continental" was a phrase that was used for a hundred years to denote worthlessness. A "Continental" was the dollar issued by the new Congress to pay for troops and supplies.

But then a winter came whose ferocity has not been repeated since, the winter of 1779–80.

One of the best descriptions of that year I have found is in the Antrim town history. The town doctor, Doctor Whiton, writes in the history that for a period of six weeks not an icicle or a single drop of water melted from the eaves of the houses.

For most of the winter the snow measured five feet on a level.

No horses could travel or even be moved from the stables. Snowshoes were the only transportation, or communication, for that matter.

Boston Harbor that year was frozen hard enough for a sleigh to ride on it.

Wood for heat had to be drawn on a hand-sled a few pieces at a time . . . and this was in a time before insulation, when it took much more wood to heat a space. Dr. Whiton tells of a small boy and his sister who cut and pulled wood this way the entire winter. Their father was at war and "having no boots, they sewed rags around their feet and saturated them with Neets foot oil to keep them from freezing."

As grain could not be transported to the grist mill, many people ran out of food and had to live on various broths and boiled corn.

In some of these deep snows, the history tells us, ordinary log houses were entirely covered and out of sight.

It would be a little over a hundred years before such a winter would be seen again and that would be the great blizzard of 1888.

With this hundred-year-or-so interval between blizzards, I'd say we are about due or maybe even overdue for another.

## Undertakers

IN THE EARLY days, death and burial were family matters. There was no such thing as embalming. The body was simply washed and laid out, often on the bed.

Burial was within a day, because, especially in the summer, a body would not keep. People often had burial grounds on their property although that required the consent of the town. Often half-a-dozen families would go in together on a graveyard.

Hills were often places where you'd find burial sites. Sometimes, for practical reasons, the spot was chosen because the digging there was not difficult.

There was usually a shroud, that is, a bag that the body would be sewn up in and placed in the grave. Sometimes there would be a homemade coffin.

Hancock, New Hampshire, had a community coffin. The body would be placed in the coffin for the service but removed at the graveyard, so the coffin could be used again for the next "dearly departed."

In Concord, the city history tells us, the first commercial coffin maker was a guy named John Johnson who made the boxes of pine boards and stained them with a bright Venetian red. There were no coffins in stock but they were made to order to the customer's size.

The coffin maker, the history tells us, had his business in the old Union Schoolhouse.

Later on, a harness maker named John Coburn came to town and made a pretty good business by taking John Johnson's simple, pine boxes and trimming them out with molding and lining them with sheeting.

This business gradually evolved into Concord's first "Undertaking and Funeral Conducting Business" which ran for a couple generations until it was sold in 1875 to Fifield and Hubbard.

Undertaker Coburn also had an apprentice who continued in the business.

Well into the twentieth century, the sign on his establishment in the Chadwick Block read simply, "J. A. Hastings, Undertaker and Harness Maker."

# The Doctor's Pay

DOCTOR EZRA CARTER was a beloved physician who lived in Nelson back during the Revolutionary War. He would administer to the sick and injured no matter their ability to pay.

There is a story in the Nelson town history in the collection entitled, "Tellable Tales."

Seems there was a family so poor that they wore rags. Disease fell on this destitute family, and Dr. Carter went many times to their hovel to treat their maladies. The family recovered and the father became distraught. How ever would he pay the doctor?

"I have been faithful to you, and am I not entitled to a reward?" the doctor asked.

"Do wait a little," the head of the household begged, "I cannot pay you now."

"I can inform you, my good friends," the doctor said, "that you have property enough to satisfy my demands and, moreover, that I shall have it before leaving the house!" The family was thunderstruck!

At that moment, a flock of kittens scampered across the room. The doctor caught one of them and put it in his pocket.

"I told you I should have my pay, and I have got it. Goodbye," he said, "and God bless you."

# *Bison Man*

BACK IN COLONIAL times, military musters were very popular. Everybody turned out to see the marching and maneuvers. But in New Ipswich in the year 1800, there was a muster that got way out of control.

Early military musters were great entertainments, much like county fairs of today. There were games of chance, sideshow exhibits, food and stuff for sale and, of course, marching bands.

The New Ipswich town history tells us that this muster was held on the Hoar farm on level ground bordering the Souhegan River. At this muster a brand-new march was introduced. It was called "The Ipswich Muster," and it was very popular and played a lot for many years thereafter.

Along with the marching, there was sham fighting and recitations and an exhibition of a bison from the Western plains. It was the bison that caused the problem that day, or at least the owner of the bison.

The town history does not tell us why the crowd was angry with him. We can only speculate that he charged too much for his exhibit. But the upshot of it all was that the mob tore down the man's shanty and let his bison loose and then, for sport, chased the man all over the field until they caught him.

The town history tells us this was great amusement, and everyone had a good time but it does not tell us what they did to the poor man after they caught him. Or what happened to his bison.

# Bear-Back Riding

NOW THIS STORY concerns a thing that certain young men did a couple hundred years ago as a feat of derring-do.

It was called bear-back riding.

Now I always thought that bareback riding was what circus performers did on horses. That riding bareback was riding without a saddle on a horse.

When I was a kid there was an old neighborhood horse owned by Don Dunklee down on Nashua Street in Milford. We used to ride bareback on the sweet old nag.

But reading a history about Swanzey, I learned that there was a thing called bear-back riding . . . that is riding on a bear's back.

The game was to discover a wild bear and bridle the beast with a cod line and see if you could stay on the critter's back.

I'm not kidding. By the way, what is a "cod line?" I guess it's a fishing line of some sort.

Anyhow here's the story as I found it in the old history published by Benjamin Reed in 1880.

The story takes place about 1800. One day General Philemon Whitcomb and his two sons, Abijah and Benjamin, were searching out old growth pine timber in the forest south of town in a place, the history tells us, called "Weare Barn."

The three were looking at the trees when they were distracted by the barking of their small dog. The history doesn't tell us what kind of a dog it was, simply that it was "little" and it was yapping.

They went to investigate and found the animal at the entrance to a cave beneath a large rock. It looked to them as if there might be a bear in there. So they gathered rocks from around the area and barricaded the entrance so the beast could not get out. Then one of the sons, Abijah, went to fetch John Grimes.

Now John Grimes was the most noted hunter in the area. He could shoot and he could trap and he knew how to dispatch a bear with an ax. So he grabbed his gun and knife and ax and started for the cave with Abijah.

At the same time the general had also departed the scene, leaving the place in charge of his other son, Benjamin. The general went home to fetch a length of cod line to make a bridle for the bear. He was a brave man and did not want the bear killed. Rather he wanted her alive for the thrill of riding, the history tells us, bear-back.

Well, the general and his cod line and the hunter with his ax arrived back at the cave about the same time.

Benjamin told them that, yes, there was a bear in the cave and she had tried to move the rocks but had failed.

So the four men set to work and uncovered the entrance to the cave and waited for the bear to come out.

It took a few minutes but come out she did, and she was a lot bigger than the men thought she would be. Out she came, rearing up on her hind legs in a ferocious manner and splitting the air with her roar.

The hunter, John Grimes, swung the ax and hit the bruin square on the back of the head with the flat end to stun the animal. That way the general could get his cod line over her muzzle and mount her back.

But the blow did little and the bear immediately turned on the hunter with her claws and teeth, and John Grimes had no other choice than to plant the blade of his weapon right in the center of the bear's head.

That, too, did little to slow her down, but she did turn and stagger a bit with the ax in the top of her head.

Right at this time, the general jumped on the animal's back even though he had not time to make a bridle. The bear was reeling by this time, but the general held on and rode her until she fell dead underneath him.

The history tells us it was not a great distance away.

And thus was the only recorded incidence of bear-back riding ever in the town of Swanzey... or maybe any other place in New Hampshire for that matter.

# The Pirate Caper

DURING THE WAR of 1812, all trade between Europe and America ceased to be, for all intents and purposes.

Both the English and the Americans supported pirate ships. They called themselves "privateers." Any ship bound for or from America was in danger. Of course because of this ceasing of trade, those ships that got through made a lot of money.

And so it was that a couple brothers from Portsmouth sent a ship to Europe and the West Indies. But coming up the coast the ship was overtaken by an American privateer. The ship was flying an American flag but, by this time, the pirates could have given a darn. They claimed the ship to be British and the flag to be false.

The crew of the ship was taken off and put in irons and a new crew was placed aboard to sail the ship into Charleston.

Left aboard the ship was the only African American member of the crew; a man from Portsmouth named John Francis.

John Francis knew every rope and plank in the ship. He was a bright and able sailor who was underestimated by the pirates because of his color. John Francis not only knew all the workings of the ship, he also knew where the gold was stored. You see, the triangle trade had gone from Portsmouth to Europe to the Caribbean and was heading home again with not only rum and sugar, but also a great number of gold coins they had received for their goods.

John Francis knew where this cache of gold was and, late that first night, he stole to the place it was hidden and took it up on deck. There on deck was an ugly greasy mess in a tub. This was renderings from animal fat that they used for what was called slushing the mast, which is adding grease to keep the ropes waterproof and the masts from splitting. The mess in the pot was disgusting and stank and was black and opaque. John Francis sank the gold coins to the bottom of this rancid mess.

When the ship arrived in port, they allowed John Francis to go. He pleaded with the crew. He said that he had nothing. Would they, he asked, allow him to take the old slush tub. The grease, he said, could be sold and would raise him a little money that he might eat a day or two. Well, the pirates thought this hysterical. They laughed and laughed as this poor black man left the ship with the disgusting mess slopping over his shoulders.

Fifteen thousand dollars in gold. He put it right in the bank. Then he made his way back to Portsmouth where he soon was reunited with the Haven brothers who were also allowed to go.

His employers were ecstatic and impressed with his daring and honesty, and they gave him money and built him a fine house on Anthony Street where John Francis lived for a few years when he was in port.

Later he moved to New Orleans where he married and had a family. The last that was heard of him, he was a clerk in a shipping company down there.

# A Toast to a Building

BACK IN THE early days of New Hampshire, it was the custom when putting up a house or other building to name the place and christen it with a cup of rum and a laudatory verse.

In 1818 in Andover, when the carpenters raised the frame of Dr. Silas Merrill's home on Taunton Hill, they broke a bottle of rum over the ridge pole and recited this verse:

> *Here is a fine frame raised on Taunton Hill*
> *The owner is rich and growing richer still*
> *May health come upon us like showers of grace*
> *And the owner gets rich by the sweat of his face.*

When they framed up the big blacksmith shop for Colonel Jonathan Weare on Taunton Hill, a guy named Samuel Keniston wrote and recited the ode for the occasion. It went:

> *Here's a fine frame raised upon a hill*
> *The owner is rich and growing richer still.*

I dunno if you noticed this, but the first two lines of this poem are almost the same as the first two lines of the poem to Dr. Merrill's house.... I guess it was convention to start these poems out this way.

Again:

> *Here's a fine frame raised upon a hill*
> *The owner is rich and growing richer still*
> *He makes very good shoes, plowshares and axes*
> *And steals enough out of his hoes to pay all his taxes.*

Anyhow, Colonel Weare was livid with Sam Keniston for this verse. When he came down from the frame, the colonel grabbed him and said, "Sam, you dog, what did you tell that lie for?"

"Oh," said Sam, "I was obliged to . . . for the rhyme."

And then he said, "I knew it was a lie when I said that you made very good shoes, plowshares and axes."

## *America's First Great Trotting Horse*

THE HISTORY OF horse racing in England began in the town of Newmarket. There were flat and round tracks where the sport of kings was practiced since the late 1500s.

But there is a historical racing story that concerns Newmarket, New Hampshire, as well.

This is one of the times where the names from the story are lost to history. All that is remembered in the Newmarket town history is the name of the horse itself. I say, "itself." The horse was a gelding.

Seems that back in the spring of 1818, a guy from Maine showed up in Newmarket to spend a few days with his cousin. His cousin was a horse breeder and farmer. The cousin from Maine had with him a trotting horse and a home-made sulky, or rather a two-wheeled cart which the horse pulled.

The cousin was dressed in homespun and looked quite seedy. His horse was strange-looking as well. It was rangy with slanting shoulders but its legs were long and strong.

Actually, the sight of the horse and his bumpkin-looking owner was quite comical. The man told his cousin that he was on his way to Boston to win the Jockey Club Prize.

See, the Boston Jockey Club had a standing offer of $1,000 to any horse that could run a mile in less than three minutes. He took his cousin out to a flat stretch of road and let the horse go. The Newmarket man was impressed.

Over the next couple days the two men cooked up a plan. Later that week the guy from Maine drove his gelding the rest of the way to Boston.

His cousin bought some fine clothes and went to Portsmouth where he took the packet to Boston. He showed up at the Jockey Club to find his cousin the brunt of much humor. He had been bragging that he had the horse to win the $1,000. (By the way, this was a time when most people made less than a hundred dollars a year. And, in fact, this was the year when the New Hampshire Legislature put a floor of thirteen dollars on what a man could owe before he became a debtor.)

So $1,000 was a dozen years' salary for most.

Anyhow, back to Boston: The cousin from Newmarket was introduced to his relative by the sports' people there at the track and the two men acted as if this were the first time they ever saw each other.

The sport from Newmarket made it known that he would put up $1,000 for the guy from Maine if the guy would put up his ownership papers on his horse as collateral. Done. And now the race was in earnest.

Everyone was laughing and betting against the nag and having a great time until the day of the race.

The horse was re-named "Boston Blue," and "Boston Blue" ran the mile in two minutes and fifty seconds. The two men won $2,000 that day and sold "Boston Blue" to the club for another $1,000.

And Boston Blue went down in racing history as the first great horse to come from America. What a story.

Boston Blue was later sold to a breeder in Boston and, get this, Boston Blue ended his days in England . . . you got it . . . in Newmarket, over there.

## Jackson in Concord

AT NOON ON June 28, 1833, Lieutenant Colonel Robert Davis arrived in his carriage at the town line between Concord and Bow.

There he found a few hundred townspeople and strangers milling about.

Colonel Davis was the chairman of the Concord Town Committee.

Soon, down the road Colonel Davis and the crowd saw a large carriage with four horses trotting their way.

A huge cheer went up. For in that carriage was the most noted and most popular man in America . . . president of the United States Andrew Jackson.

With the president was Vice President Martin Van Buren who was himself to be next in line for the presidency.

There on the town line Colonel Davis stood on the rear of his wagon and gave a welcoming speech to the president.

A great cavalcade formed and marched with the president to the Plain of Concord where they were joined by eight companies of militia, under the command of Colonel Stephen Peabody of Milford.

President Jackson got out of his barouche and mounted a beautiful horse and led the procession into town . . . down Main Street, down State Street, and across School Street. The city history estimates that more than 10,000 people were there cheering their hero.

The president then dismounted and went to his quarters at the Eagle House. He was very tired. You may know his body was a mass of war and dueling wounds, and even carried musket bullets which doctors of the time could not remove. He retired early.

Next morning he reviewed Colonel Peabody's troops. The display ended with the troops forming two lines of men to make a passageway from the Eagle House to the Statehouse.

Picture this . . . down the walkway the president walked with the governor and several former governors along with the vice president and lots of military and retired military men, including the secretary of war and the secretary of the Navy.

A huge cheer went up in Representatives Hall as the president entered. He shook hands with all the state senators.

Later that day he visited the New Hampshire State Prison and afterwards attended a social put on by some 500 Concord ladies. The history says the ladies were thrilled.

Next day was Sunday and the president attended parts of services in all the churches... Unitarian, Methodist, Baptist and Congregational.

He met two teenage boys who had been named for him... Isaac Andrew Hill and Andrew Jackson Hill.

He gave each a silver coin saying it was "the eagle of his country which in all his life he had endeavored to defend. Keep it," he said, "in remembrance of me."

The next morning Colonel Davis and his committee escorted the president back to the Bow town line where they had met him three days before. There the president dismounted his horse... took off his hat and shook hands all around.

He then got in his carriage and rode off into the dust.

# *The Horse Boat*

GUNDALOWS WERE THE way goods were transported on Great Bay and down the Salmon and Piscataqua rivers between Portsmouth and Dover and Exeter years ago.

The gundalow was a single-masted, scow-like work boat indigenous, we are told, to the region. Apparently the name was a mispronunciation of "gondola."

But did you know that they used gundalows to move goods on Lake Winnipesaukee as well? Well, they did.

It was the railroad that spelled death for the gundalow on Great Bay and, according to the Gilford town history, it was the horse boat that spelled the death of the gundalow on the lake.

Now I didn't say, "houseboat." I said, "horse boat." And if you have never heard of a "horse boat," you are not alone. Horse boats were only a passing phenomenon, soon replaced by steam engines.

But Winnipesaukee had one of the first and most famous horse boats.

The craft was invented by a guy named Patten down in Manchester back in 1837. He made his prototype from boards cut from trees on Governor's Island.

Like the gundalow, the horse boat was sort of a flat scow about seventy feet long. The craft had machinery that turned a paddle wheel which was, in turn, moved by a treadmill that had two horses on it. The machinery was made in a foundry down in Lake Village by Squire John Barron and his partner, a man named Parsons.

Did it work? You bet it did! In the first year, the history tells us, it managed to glut the market for green firewood in Lake Village. The boat could carry twenty cords of wood in a single sailing.

Soon the horse boat was moving cotton bales and lumber and supplies for the mills.

In the summer of 1841, a man named Smith was piloting the craft with a load of goods from Alton Bay bound for Lake Village. Aboard were fifteen tons of iron bars, half a dozen bales of cotton, flour, dyestuff and other goods. They were on their way when a sudden storm came up the lake.

The boat did not capsize but it did tip and the cotton bales floated away. Captain Smith could not control his unwieldy craft and finally had to beach it on the rocky shore.

No one said it at the time, but it seems he could have used more horsepower.

## The Great Awakening

BETWEEN THE REVOLUTIONARY and Civil Wars, a religious revival took hold in England and America. It was called "The Second Great Awakening."

In New Hampshire there were traveling evangelists who turned out thousands for meetings in tents and town halls.

In the 1840s in Benton, New Hampshire, a number of incidents brought people to their churches.

The town history notes that Elder Cogswell spoke at a funeral of one who had died of diphtheria. He is quoted as saying, "They are having diphtheria up my way and the young folks are scared and are getting religion."

By the way, Elder Cogswell had a remedy for diphtheria. It was made of West Indian molasses, cayenne pepper and salt pork.

David Norris of Benton attended a revival meeting and was not moved, the history tells us. Later in the summer he was clearing some land with Ira Whitcher. It was a very hot day and it was made hotter by the burning pile of wood that the men had dragged from the clearing.

David mused on the fire and then turned and said, "According to some folks tell, Ira, I s'pose hell's just as much hotter than that as you can think. But damned if I believe it. A man couldn't live in it two minutes."

Once when a revival preacher came to Benton, a couple of hell-raising young men came by to hoot and disrupt the proceedings. Their names were Bill Bacon and his pal Ben Eliot.

They came to scoff but Bill got caught up in the preacher's words and gave himself over to the Lord right there on the spot. The town history tells us that he got under a deep conviction. That he prayed and went to the mourners' bench and was converted.

Right off though, he became anxious about his friend, Ben. And he prayed aloud and this is what he said, "Oh, Lord, there is a great sinner here tonight. Ben Elliot. If he dies before morning he'll surely go to hell, which favor we ask. Amen."

For the sake of his soul, Ben, too, was converted that night.

# Webster Comes Back to Portsmouth

NO DOUBT YOU know that Daniel Webster lived in Portsmouth from 1807 to 1816. It was there that he married Grace Fletcher. He was twenty-five at the time and had his law offices upstairs in a building on Market Street.

He and Grace were blissfully happy then. They lived first in a house on Vaughn Street that stood just about to the left of where the Blue Mermaid is today.

Two years later, Daniel Webster had become quite successful, and he and his family moved to a home on Pleasant Street. And the Websters probably would have stayed in Portsmouth if it hadn't been for the great fire of 1813.

This terrible fire burned most of the downtown of the city including the Webster house. He was not insured and suffered terrible losses. Three years later the family moved to Boston. And that was the end of Daniel Webster's association with the Granite State.

But he never forgot us. In his old age he reminisced about the happiness of his youth . . . especially with his young family and Grace in Portsmouth. Grace, by the way, was to die after nineteen years with the great man.

But Daniel Webster returned to Portsmouth often. And the last time was on May 17, 1844. That day he came back to Portsmouth accompanying the delegation that had just nominated Henry Clay for president in Baltimore.

Clay, by the way, lost the election to the Democrat James K. Polk. He lost because he opposed the annexation of Texas as a slave state. This stand cost him the support of the South. Anyhow, I digress.

In 1844 when Webster returned for the last time to the port city, he was sixty-two years old. The citizens gave him a reception at Jefferson Hall. Jefferson Hall used to sit at the north and east end of Pleasant Street about where the sidewalk widens going into Market Square.

At the gathering Webster met with old friends (those who were still alive). Most, alas, were not. In fact, he began his address by saying, "Your fathers . . . were my associates. And my friends."

He went on to say, "The future is not within our power. No man knows what is assigned to be his lot. Human life is uncertain. Human destiny is unknown. But we have a country which will be spared for future generations. Human life is short. But institutions of government should be made to endure."

Daniel Webster stayed in the hall until he had spoken with all who wished to speak with him and shaken hands with all who wished to shake his hand. Before he left he said to the group, "The nine years of the most active portion of my life spent here are treasured in my heart with my dearest, my most-enduring recollections," and here tears trickled down his cheek and checked his utterance for he knew it would be the last time he would be there.

Daniel Webster died on October 12, 1852, at his home in Marshfield, Massachusetts.

And, yes, he never did get back to Portsmouth.

# The Bridegroom Doth Not Come

THIS IS AN unsolved mystery that Charles Brewster tells of in his historical book, *Rambles about Portsmouth*. The story takes place in Portsmouth in the 1860s.

Seems Jacob Sheaf had a beautiful daughter, Abigail. She had older brothers and lots of suitors.

One of the suitors was James McDonough. James had come to Portsmouth from England about 1857 with a small amount of capital and had opened an English goods store over near Bow Street. Jim McDonough had a knack for business and in ten years he had prospered. His prices were good, and he had a reputation for being fair.

He was now a member of Portsmouth society. He was even elected as an officer in St. John's Lodge, a great honor. His success made him bold and, in 1868, he asked Abigail for her hand ... and she accepted.

The wedding was to be held at the home of the bride. The evening for the nuptials arrived and all of Portsmouth society was there. The table groaned under the weight of imported fruits and sweetmeats. The minister was there. The bride was there. The bride's family was there ... their friends. But the groom failed to appear.

Whether he ran away or met with foul play is not known to this day. But the wedding was off.

For years people speculated about the event. Most of the town thought he ran away. But he had borrowed money from Colonel George Boyd and, when he could not be found, James McDonough's entire fortune reverted to the colonel, making him, by far, the richest man in Portsmouth.

All the bride-to-be received were a few pieces of silverware.

Abigail Sheafe, by the way, did not languish. She fell in love again. This time with the Honorable John Pickering. The couple lived in a fine house and had many children.

# Manchester Log Run

AH, THE ROMANCE of the log drives. The lumberjacks dancing over the floating logs as they float down the Ammonoosuc and the Androscoggin. Logs on their way to the sawmill.

But where were these sawmills?

In Maine they were often on the coast where the lumber could be put right on a ship.

But one of the largest sawmills in New England back in the nineteenth century was the Norcross Company. And the Norcross Company was located in Lowell, Massachusetts.

Yes, Lowell. And that meant that each spring there was a stupendous log drive right through Manchester . . . on the Merrimack River. For fifty years, from 1847 to 1897, each spring, there was a log run through Manchester.

When the freshet came, the logs would be floated down to the holding place just above Amoskeag Falls. Here a temporary boom was strung across the river. See, you couldn't just let the logs spill over the falls willy-nilly or higgledy-piggledy. Oh no, that would have created a pick-up-straws clog of tremendous proportions there at the base of the falls. No lumber at all would have gotten down to Lowell.

The men would camp right beside the river in tents. These were skilled workers and they got good pay. They were also glamorous. They all wore red shirts. They placed their lives in jeopardy every day. They were bachelors (or at least miles from their wives). And they were great dancers. This was because they were so agile dancing on the floating logs.

The Manchester young ladies always looked forward to the coming of the "Knockies."

They were called "Knockies" because they were employed by the Norcross Company.

At the break of morning, the Knockies would start floating the logs over the falls. This was spring, and there was a tremendous amount of water coming down the river. Most of the logs got over but there were always half a dozen times when there was what was called "a glut." A glut was a pile up of logs at the base of the falls.

The boss would shout, "Who breaks this glut?" and the volunteers would run out on the mess dancing on the spinning logs. There they would pry the logs apart with their peavies, the wooden tools they used for balance and handling. When the mass began to break apart, someone would yell, "Run in!" and everyone would run across the logs for shore. This was the most dangerous time, and every year someone would be seriously injured or killed at Amoskeag.

And yet there was great good humor among these men. In the evening they would sit by their campfires and sing, and many people from Manchester would come by just to sit and listen.

# Frost Free Library

*Rufus Frost was the patron of the Marlborough library.*

SOME OF THE people in the town of Marlborough, New Hampshire, got together back in 1795 and established a social library.

The library was available to people of the town for fifty years. But then it fell into disuse just before the Civil War.

During the war a lot of Americans got rich, especially in the North. And one of these people was lawyer named Rufus Frost. Mr. Frost lived in Chelsea, Massachusetts, but he had been born in Marlborough. He spent his first six years in this town. And then his father died, and he went to live with relatives.

But over the years Rufus Frost had come back to Marlborough each summer to be in the shadow of Monadnock Mountain and to breathe the country air.

He loved Marlborough and respected its people.

And so in 1865, he wrote to the town to say that he intended to give to the town a free public library.

He realized that the Civil War had left most people in hard straights and he would not think of having the town increase its taxation for his gift and so he was also including an endowment for the library's upkeep and for purchases of books. The cost, including construction and endowment, would come to $5,000. All the town had to do was donate a piece of land.

And so it was that on August 28, 1867, the entire town was at the beautiful granite building to accept the gift and thank their benefactor. There was a parade with the Keene Brass Band and a huge picnic and fireworks and speeches and, generally, everyone had a great time.

And as the keys to the building were delivered to the town, the inscription was unveiled to reveal that the town had named their new possession after the benefactor himself.

I just love the name.

This is the Frost Free Library.

I wonder if they have a frost-free refrigerator in there.

## *The Five Trees*

IN THE EIGHTEENTH and nineteenth centuries, epidemic outbreaks of smallpox and spotted fever were regular occurrences.

When this happened, the victims were segregated into pesthouses.

These places were often abandoned houses and farms on the outskirts of towns where people with the diseases were quarantined from their families and townspeople.

Even doctors stayed away except in cases of very important people, and the victims were left to nurse each other. Food would be left at the doorstep by friends and family.

In Gilford, according to the town history, there were two outbreaks of spotted fever ... one in 1827 and another forty-six years later, in 1873.

The Gilford pesthouse was located on Goodwin Road, near the Gunstock Brook in a farmhouse that had been unoccupied for a number of years.

In the second outbreak, the story goes, five brothers were confined to the pesthouse, and all died of the disease.

A dozen years later, the legend goes, the old farm caught fire and burned to the ground. Only the foundation filled with ashes was left.

From these ashes, it is said, five trees grew. These, people said, were the souls of the five brothers.

This may be folklore only, but the fact is there are five graves in the field behind the old foundation.

# Transatlantic Cable

NOWADAYS YOU CAN talk to just about anyone, at any time, and from anywhere.

I e-mailed a friend of mine in England last night and got an e-mail back from him this morning. On TV the announcer talks back and forth with people in Afghanistan.

Now there is a reason I am waxing philosophic about all this, and the reason has to do with the historic ground where the very first direct transatlantic cable came ashore in the United States.

It happened in (and this may surprise you) 1874.

Now words are important here. I say, this was the first cable coming directly from Europe to the United States. There had, in fact, been transatlantic cables before, but they went to Canada; usually Newfoundland. There the messages were translated and re-sent via overland telegraph to their destinations in the United States.

But the first cable, with one end in Europe and the other end in the United States, came into the country in Rye, New Hampshire.

The Rye town history records the day the cable was brought ashore.

It was July 15, a Wednesday. It was hot. The sea was as calm as anyone had seen it. The cable itself had touched shore at Halifax, Nova Scotia. From there it went along the sea bottom down the coast to a position off the Isles of Shoals.

The steamer *Ambassador* was to lay the short piece of cable from the Isles of Shoals to a point off Locke's Neck.

The cable had been planned to come ashore the day before and a thousand people had gathered to see the momentous event. But things took longer than was expected.

On Wednesday morning, two steam-launches carried the shore section of the cable to a platform on the shore. The reel of cable weighed 15 tons.

At three o'clock in the afternoon, the shore end of the cable was successfully landed. People on the shore took hold of a rope tied to the cable and to the high water mark. The town history records that even the ladies helped tow the line.

A hundred-gun salute was then fired by a contingent from Kittery that had brought two small cannons for that purpose. The steamer Ambassador echoed the salute. Rockets were sent up from the ship. Everyone cheered.

At nine o'clock that night the *Ambassador* weighed anchor and sailed toward the Isles of Shoals, there to pick up the main cable and make the splice.

It was September before the first messages were sent, but they went directly from Rye, New Hampshire, to Ballenskelligs, Ireland, a distance of over 2,500 nautical miles. No stops. And thus, the first electronic messages from the United States sent directly to Europe were sent from a little town on the coast of New Hampshire.

The company, by the way, was completely owned by the Brits, and they sent their own people to man the station there.

There were four men on at all times, two sending, two receiving messages in Morse code. The sender mechanism was what is called a double key, and the receiver was a mirror galvanometer which employed a mirror hung from a cat hair that reflected a light off the wall which greatly amplified the movement of the mirror.

The cable worked until 1913 when, because of the First World War, the British were strapped for money and unable to maintain the cable.

If you scuba dive off this shore you may have noticed the cable is still there.

# Kinky Schoolteacher

IN APRIL OF 1878, the town of Milford held a big party to celebrate the new town hall to which only people fifty years old and older were invited. Two hundred and eighty-nine people showed up.

Back then the old town hall was Eagle Hall, so-called because of the eagle on the top of the cupola. But the party was held in the brand new town hall on a corner of Nashua Street.

At noon, the Milford Cornet Band played, and the oldsters marched out of the Eagle Hall and once around the town common and into the new town hall. There was much cheering.

Inside there was a dinner presided over by the Honorable Timothy Kaley. John W. Pillsbury was the toastmaster. Those are both historic names in Milford. Today there is the Kaley Prize Speaking Contest and the Kaley Auditorium and the Pillsbury Home for the aged and Pillsbury State Park up in Washington.

Anyhow, Asa Merrill, the first child born in Milford after its incorporation, was called on to rise and received prolonged cheers. The crowd also cheered the oldest person in town, 88-year-old Clausia Towne.

Poems were read and one of the old-timers, one Samuel Lovejoy, told this story:

> My father moved his family to Milford in 1794. Came in an ox cart.
>
> We lived in what is now the Osgood District, in which there were, in 1810, thirteen framed and three log houses.
>
> Most of the traveling was done in ox-carts, there being but two two-wheeled carriages in town. People generally went to the mill on horseback.
>
> Barrels of rum were drunk in those days; ministers and mourners used it freely at funerals. Ministers' salaries ranged from three hundred to four hundred dollars a year.
>
> I remember a school teacher who tied up her future husband in the stanchions of a barn and flogged him.

So there you go. History doesn't have to be dull.

# Dynamite Corner

IT HAPPENED OVER a hundred and twenty years ago at a crossroads in the town of Strafford . . . out near the Crown Point Baptist Church.

There used to be an old Georgian house on the east corner of the place, a farmhouse belonging to an eighty-three-year-old man named Stephen Young.

Old Mr. Young lived there with his daughter, Mary Ann, another young woman named Sadie Greenfield, and a seventeen-year-old girl from an orphanage in Lowell who did chores around the place.

Back in the summer of 1883 the well on the property went dry and so that winter Stephen Young hired a young man and a couple helpers to dig a new well.

The well digger was a guy named Taylor Berry who had been out in the gold fields of California for a few years and thus had some experience digging in the earth.

Right off, Berry and his two assistants, George Goodwin and Joseph May, ran into trouble. Under the land near the house it was all ledge and no way to get through it.

Well, Stephen Young knew of a young man who could, he said, handle dynamite. This man was twenty-five-year-old George Young of Lowell. The town history doesn't say so, but George Young may have been part of Stephen Young's family. Either way old Steve sent for young George and also some dynamite.

Problem was that it was against the law to transport dynamite through the mails or over the railroads for that matter. The American Express Company expressly (no pun intended) excluded any hazardous material from their deliveries. That included gasoline, naphtha and gun powder. They even refused to carry matches.

Well, old Steve and young George got round this by packing the dynamite in a laundry basket from Lowell with the laundry's name stenciled on the outside.

Sure enough, one January day the laundry basket arrived at the railroad station in Rochester, and Charlie Parsons, the driver for

American Express, put it in his wagon and urged his horse on to the Young farm. He had no idea what he was carrying.

At the farm they took the dynamite inside because it froze easier than water and, to be effective, it had to be warmed.

George Young put it on a shelf behind the wood stove and began rigging up a homemade detonator made out of wire and a couple dry cell batteries. Problem was, he couldn't get the thing to spark. The other workmen were scared to death and wouldn't stay in the house while George was fiddling around with the thing.

About suppertime, old Stephen Young was sitting in the parlor conversing with Sadie Greenfield. His daughter Mary Ann was in a room next to the kitchen where George Young was working on the dynamite detonator.

The three men digging the well came to the door and said that they would not come into supper unless George stopped work on the detonator. He agreed. The men came in and started washing up for supper. But George couldn't help himself and he tried his device once more.

What happened next was that the entire bottom half of that big old farmhouse was blown apart.

The hired girl was at the stove. She was blown into what was left of the dining room. Later they found her under a heavy timber. Her face was badly burned, and she carried the scars for the rest of her life. But she survived.

The old man, Stephen Young, was blown into the parlor but was unhurt. Miss Greenfield, who was in the living room with him at the time of the explosion, was blown clear through the walls and about fifty feet into the woods. She sustained a bad cut to her face but she too recovered.

Stephen's daughter Mary Ann was discovered outside the kitchen under the debris horribly burned and broken. She died three days later. Her last words were: "I told him not to fool with it."

The laborer, George Goodwin was able to walk away from the blast and seemed unharmed. Sitting at the kitchen table in the house next door, however, he told the neighbor, "I am bleeding inside. I am going to die." And he was right. He died that evening.

The other laborer, Joe May, was found in the cellar, badly burned and delirious. He survived but lost his eyesight in one eye.

The guy who set the whole thing off, George Young, had his pants and underwear blown off and his lower extremities were badly burned. But he survived and later married Sadie Greenfield, the gal who was talking with old Stephen when the blast went off.

The man originally hired to dig the well, Taylor Berry, was discovered in the ruins behind the kitchen. He was also badly burned and paralyzed from the waist down. He lived three years more but finally succumbed to his injuries. His father sued the Youngs and got a settlement of five thousand dollars.

This is the tombstone he put up for his son. It reads:

> *Here lies my darling only son*
> *Caused by a rebel whose name is Young.*
>
> *Z.T. Berry Died Sept. 8, 1887 age 36 years, 17 days.*

Oh, and by the way, the crossroads there in Strafford has, ever since the explosion, been called . . . Dynamite Corners.

# Prices in 1895

HOW MUCH HAVE you spent this week? A lot, I'll bet.

All of us remember the good old days. How "good old" depends on how old we are. The older we get the more "good old" they get.

Coffee cost a nickel a cup until I was in my twenties. Pay phone was a nickel too. Coke was a nickel, and Pepsi used to advertise that it gave you double the amount of cola that Coke did for that same nickel.

In the Milford town history there is a paragraph about what it cost to live back in 1895.

The year 1895 is important because there was a depression and apparently things had never been cheaper; at least that's what it says in the history. Anyhow, here's what the history tells us:

"The best St. Louis flour is sold at four dollars a barrel; butter is twenty to thirty cents a pound. Potatoes are forty cents a bushel; salt pork, eight cents a pound; sugar, five cents a pound.

"Yard wide cotton sheeting is seven cents a yard; calico is five-to-eight cents a yard.

"Kerosene is twelve cents a gallon. Workhorses sell for an average of a hundred dollars each. Ready-made clothing has never sold at a lower price. Anthracite coal sells for six dollars a ton and a cord of wood is four dollars. ('Course that cord of wood was, no doubt, hand hewn and sawn.)"

Actually those low prices were not as cheap as you might think. Laborers made a dollar and a half to two dollars a day back in 1895 . . . seven to ten dollars a week was a darned good wage.

A working person today makes maybe forty times that. So that five cents a pound for sugar back then translates to four dollars a pound today and a pound of butter would be about ten bucks.

It's been said before but I can't resist saying it again: "These . . . these are the 'good old days.'"

# *Trashin'*

THERE IS A sort of tradition in regard to some rock 'n roll bands that they should trash hotel rooms and smash instruments on stage. It seems like a recent phenomenon . . . but, of course, it isn't.

Take for instance this story that comes from the book, *Reminiscences of Lebanon*, which is a collection of stories by various people who lived in the town back in the 1930s.

This story concerns two young men who came through Lebanon back in the late 1800s.

The young men came from families of some means. They arrived at a local tavern in a light carriage, a chaise. One of the young men was obviously drunk, as he was staggering and had a slurred speech. The second young man appeared not to be drunk but he was, the history tells us, big.

The two stepped into the bar room and did not order drinks. Rather, they began to throw the furniture around. There was, the story goes, no provocation but high spirits as the two smashed chairs on the floor and destroyed tables, mirrors, windows.

A young boy, a kid named Hinkley Buswell, went into the bar to see what the commotion was and he was picked up and thrown out the window where he landed in the midst of the trash, his pride wounded but otherwise unhurt.

By this time, the two men were smashing all the bottles of liquor behind the bar. Soon the floor was covered with broken glass and whiskey and gin and rum. Lastly they smashed up the bar . . . all but a corner post which would not come loose from the floor even when the very large young man slammed against it with his shoulder and kicked at it with his feet.

The young men then called for the landlord, Moses Greenough. Landlord Greenough appeared and the two bowed to him and wrote on a piece of paper where he could send the bill for their destruction. They then bowed deeply and bid him a pleasant "Goodbye," boarded their chaise and drove toward Vermont, laughing as they went out of sight.

To the surprise of Landlord Greenough the bill was paid at once.

The story goes on to say that one of the young men was from New Hampshire and the other from Vermont and that their mothers did not know they were out and their fathers didn't care.

The young inebriated man was Willis Lyman who became a noted lawyer in Burlington, Vermont.

His friend, the very large young man, was James Wilson. Wilson grew up to become a general in the Army and later an influential member of the New Hampshire Legislature.

Such were the hijinks of some children of the rich in an earlier time.

## Stop the Wedding!

ON WEDNESDAY, DECEMBER 12, 1906, William Dion and Elizabeth Ryan joined hands in front of the Rev. Dr. Cyrus Richardson in the parlor of Mr. Ryan's home on Grove Street in Nashua.

"Dearly beloved," Reverend Richardson intoned, "we are gathered here today in the sight of God and this company to join this man and this . . . ."

But before the ceremony could go any further, a policeman appeared and yelled, "Stop the wedding!"

The police officer was Horace Ballou. He had been sent to the groom's home by Nashua Chief of Police Wheeler who had been asked to stop the wedding by the bride's mother and stepfather.

The bride, the mother said, was only sixteen years old and the groom was . . . horror of horrors . . . a divorced man.

They would not give their permission for their girl to marry such a person.

See, this was a hundred years ago and a divorce was not a common occurrence.

Well, the minister was non-plused and bright red. What a scandal. What if the board of directors of the Congregational Church heard about this!

He skedaddled.

The fifty or so guests at the wedding were also upset. They wanted the wedding done so they could eat.

The bride sank into the arms of her husband-to-be, and Officer Ballou ordered the two of them to accompany him to the police station. Not without a warrant, you damned fool, the groom said. So Officer Ballou returned to the station house alone to await further instructions from his chief.

In the meantime the police had called City Solicitor I. C. Eaton to get a legal opinion about the case.

Solicitor Eaton knew all about the matter. He had, in fact, represented the groom in his recent divorce. He was a friend, although not invited to the wedding.

The age of consent to get married back in 1906 was sixteen and the bride met this requirement.

The police had no business in this matter.

The bride's mother and sister had, by this time, arrived again at the station to urge the law to stop the nuptials.

They were told the marriage could not legally be stopped. The two women burst into tears and went home.

Officer Ballou was again sent to the groom's home, this time to apologize and inform everyone that the wedding could proceed.

He was met at the door by the bride and groom waving a marriage license. They had, in fact, called on another minister, the Rev. Francis O. Tyler of Hudson, who had come right over and done the service. He was, by the way, a Methodist.

Everyone was, by this time, well fed and half in the bag. They invited Officer Ballou to have a drink.

But he was still on duty and he had made enough mistakes that day.

# Dying

MANY OF US think the world is over regulated these days.

When I was growing up, all the kids swam at the abandoned granite quarries in my town of Milford.

Yeah, it was dangerous, and yeah, some kids died by diving into shallow water. But, back then, people took it as a part of life.

Nowadays all the quarries in Milford are posted and fenced and no one swims in them. If anyone died, there would be such lawsuits . . . attractive nuisance, is what they call it.

OSHA regulates the workplace nowadays, but back then there were no regulations. I remember seeing them take out a guy who had just lost an arm at the old Box Factory in Wilton. That was about 1953. What sadness.

Kids burned themselves with fireworks. There were lots of firearm accidents. The seat belt hadn't been invented for cars then, although safety glass had. My dad remembered when car windshields were made from simple window glass.

In Jaffrey back in the fall of 1901, a guy named Dennis Provençal worked at the White Brothers Cotton Mill as a laborer. Mr. Provençal was the son of Octave Provençal, and he lived near his dad down on Cross Street in the section of town called "Little Canada." All the people who lived there came from up north and spoke only French in their community.

Anyhow, Dennis Provençal was at work and was reaching across an area when he lost his footing and fell into a vat of boiling dye. His coworkers pulled him out with a pole but he was in great pain and stripped himself of his clothing and ran for his home. People on the street were horrified to see a wild-eyed man dyed blue-black howling and running through the streets.

There is not a happy ending to this tale. Dennis Provençal died in great pain twelve hours later.

I noted at the start of this story that many of us think that we are over regulated nowadays.

Every time I think that way, though, I remember Dennis Provençal, and I think maybe . . . maybe, it ain't so bad nowadays.

# Old Grey Bonnet

*When Mr. and Mrs. Foss left their Madbury
home for a trip to Dover, a song was born.*

TWO HUNDRED AND fifty years ago a house was built in Madbury that has, over the years, been a farm and a tavern. Nowadays, the University of New Hampshire uses it for housing..

But there is a story that is told about the house that is worth retelling.

The story takes place in 1908. Seems two songwriters from New York were visiting friends in Dover and they were put up at this house, then owned by Julia and Marshall Foss.

The songwriters were Percy Wenrich and Stanley Murphy. Wenrich had written "We Were Sailing Along on Moonlight Bay," and the pair had composed "Be My Little Baby Bumble Bee... buzz around."

Anyhow the Fosses had a son, Fred. Fred was also a musician and he played on a melodeon organ, which the family had in their parlor.

Now this story may be apocryphal but it is a good story anyway so I'll tell it:

The story goes that while Wenrich and Murphy were guests at the Foss home, Marshall Foss appeared at the door one day and asked his wife if she knew what day it was.

"Tuesday," she said.

"Yes," Marshall said, "it is Tuesday, and it is also our golden wedding anniversary. I'll hitch up the horse, and we'll drive over to Dover to the church where we were married fifty years ago."

The church was, incidentally, the old Baptist Church in the center of town. There is a Dunkin Donuts there nowadays.

That being said, Mrs. Foss got her old bonnet, and the couple started off.

And, legend has it, the two songwriters went to the melodeon and knocked out one of the greatest sing-along songs ever written, a song that I always thought of as being English. But the Dover in this song is not about Dover, England. It's about Dover, New Hampshire. And this, of course, is the verse:

> *Put on your old grey bonnet*
> *With blue ribbons on it,*
> *And we'll hitch old dobbin to the shay,*
> *Over fields of clover*
> *We will drive to Dover*
> *On our Golden Wedding Day.*

# Lithium Spring

AT THE TURN of the twentieth century, people would travel miles to "take the waters," as they called it.

What that meant was going to a spa or a hotel to drink from some sort of mineral spring.

In Jaffrey Center there was an inn by the side of the road where the spring water was full of sulpher. It smelled like rotten eggs. People from all over came there to drink the foul-smelling stuff because . . . it obviously was medicine, medicine that God himself offered.

Everyone agreed they felt better after drinking the stuff.

Another popular New Hampshire mineral spring was at a hotel over in Bradford.

France has Perrier; Germany, Baden, and New York, Saratoga Springs. England has Bath.

But at one time there was no spring in the entire world with any more renown than a spring that used to be in Temple, New Hampshire.

And, let me tell you, this is a naughty, naughty story.

The spring was located down on the shoulder of Temple Mountain, out in the woods. There was a picnic grove with huge pine trees and a playground with seesaws and swings and slides for the kids. There was a baseball field and a gazebo. And it was all free to anyone who lived in the town of Temple . . . courtesy of Sidney Scammon and his partner and uncle, Rodney Killum.

The lovely area was supported by the mineral spring it surrounded; a spring owned by Sidney and Rodney; a spring which had, the world knew, the highest natural concentration of lithium of any spring in the entire world.

Now lithium is a useful drug. To this day it is prescribed for depression. Back then it was also thought to be good for rheumatism, dyspepsia, diabetes, eczema . . . you name it.

Wagonloads of this remarkable water were hauled out of the spring, bottled, and sent all over America. Temple was famous. And everyone loved Sidney Scammon and Uncle Rodney Killum.

That is . . . that is, until 1911.

In 1911, a newspaper reporter in Fitchburg, Massachusetts, found out something scandalous. Fitchburg, by the way, was where the lithium water was put aboard railroad cars to go all over the country. Anyhow, this reporter learned that Sidney Scammon was buying lithium in great quantities and adding it to the water!

The secret was out; there was no lithium at all in the lithium spring. Never was any lithium there.

Scammon was the perfect name for Sidney, 'cause he certainly was scamming the public.

Well, that's about the story. Both men had to leave town. It was saddest for Uncle Rodney Killum who was eighty-three years old and had lived his whole life in Temple.

The spring and the picnic area were sold and Delcie Bean and Merrill Simond of Jaffrey moved their portable sawmill in and cut down all the ancient trees.

The spring itself has been bulldozed over and today there is nothing left.

# President Wilson at Harlakenden

THE BESTSELLING AMERICAN author Winston Churchill was forever being confused with the British statesman Winston Churchill. They were, of course, two different people.

The American Churchill lived in Cornish, New Hampshire, from the late 1880s until his death in 1940.

In Cornish, he built a grand mansion overlooking the Connecticut River. He called his estate after his wife's maiden name "Harlakenden House." Mrs. Churchill had formerly been Mabel Harlakenden Hall.

The architect Charles Platt designed the house. It was elegant and very comfortable. Churchill wrote some of his most popular novels at Harlakenden House; among them, "The Crisis," "The Chronicle" and "Coniston."

In 1913, President Woodrow Wilson and his wife were looking for a respite from the heat of Washington, D.C. Mrs. Wilson was in ill health and needed fresh air.

A family friend, Norman Hapgood, had a summer place in Cornish and had learned that Harlakenden House was available for rent that year. He recommended the place to the Wilsons, and the Wilsons, solely on this recommendation and sight unseen, moved there for the summer.

They were not disappointed. The house was all it was toted to be. Mrs. Wilson was comfortable. The air was fresh and cool. And her daughters were delighted with the social life in the Cornish art colony. There were masques and concerts, dances and parties every night all summer long.

The family came back again the next year. But then Mrs. Wilson died.

President Wilson was not one to waste time, however. The next year, that is, the summer of 1915, he invited a new friend to Harlakenden House, Mrs. Edith Bolling Galt, a friend of the President's niece, Helen Wilson.

Mrs. Galt was a wealthy widow and had a bit of a reputation. Before she met the president, it was rumored, she had had an affair with the German ambassador, Count Von Bernsdorf. This was just before World War I. Von Bernsdorf, by the way, had summered in Dublin, New Hampshire, in 1914 and 1915. Dublin was the other art colony in New Hampshire. In fact, many artists went back and forth between the two artistic centers.

Nonetheless, that summer Woodrow Wilson was smitten. And Mrs. Galt was willing. So in the summer of 1915 (while Von Bernsdorf was in Dublin), Mrs. Galt and cousin Helen visited the Wilson daughters in Harlakenden. She was there when the president arrived. Everyone in the community knew what was going on.

Mrs. Galt had, the locals said, refused the president's offer of marriage because of the hubbub that surrounded the office. Later she did, of course, marry him, but that summer they just fooled around.

Mrs. Galt later wrote:

> Cornish is a charming spot, a Mecca for artists and cultivated people. The chief rivalry among these delightful folk seemed to be who could make the loveliest garden.
>
> Whenever my thoughts turn back to that wonderful summer, there seems about it all a halo of gorgeous color from the flowers, and music made by the river where nearly every day we walked when the president was there.
>
> He was like a boy home from school when he could steal a weekend away from Washington and could come there to the peace and quiet of the hills.

So it was . . . and so it is still in Cornish but not at Harlakenden.

For Harlakenden was to catch fire in 1923. Nothing of it remains.

# *Yankee Pride*

THIS IS A story I found in Ernest Poole's wonderful book titled, *The Great White Hills of New Hampshire* published by Doubleday back in 1946.

The story concerns a Yankee family living up north of the notches in Coos County in the 1920s.

Yankees, of course, have a reputation for being miserly and mean-spirited. But, being a Yankee myself, I can state unequivocally that if there is one trait that unites us, it is pride. The worst thing you can do to us is to come to our aid if we hadn't asked you to.

Pride.

Now, to the story. Seems there was an old couple living up near Colebrook, and the husband up and died one night.

Back then all funerals were held in the home and the undertaker came there to prepare the body.

Funerals were important. There was a way to do a funeral. If the funeral was done wrong, a person lost the most important thing, his or her pride. Things had to be done right.

Well, in this case the undertaker had taken sick and sent in his place his young apprentice. The family doctor also was there. They laid the old gentleman out on the bed...washed the body and trimmed the scraggy beard...pressed his only suit and put it on him...tied up his tie. In the end, you never saw a prettier corpse.

But then the widow came screaming into the room. "The funeral is in an hour," she wailed, "and I can't find my teeth!"

Well, the young undertaker went looking, and they were nowhere to be found.

"I swear they were in the kitchen," the old lady cried.

The young man found the doctor. "She can't find her teeth," he told him.

"Her teeth?" the doctor said. And they both whirled around and looked at the husband who appeared to be smiling.

In a cold sweat the doctor and the undertaker searched the old man's room and, sure enough, found his teeth.

The undertaker went out to the kitchen with the widow to search the room once more and the doctor took her teeth out of the dead man and put his in. He then dropped the choppers into alcohol to sterilize them and went out to the kitchen to give them to her.

Such relief.

"Now," the old woman said, "I won't have to shame him at his funeral."

And she smiled. The two men also smiled . . . not genuine smiles, but smiles nonetheless.

# The Klan in Charlestown

IN THE SPRING of 1915, the great American film director D.W. Griffith released his amazing Civil War epic, *The Birth of a Nation.*

In the history of entertainment up to that time no one had ever seen anything as stunning or as moving.

Viewed today (and, yes, I have seen it) the movie seems silly. The acting is old-fashioned silent movie acting... lots of bug eyes and chest thumping. The pacing is ponderous.

But back then, even President Woodrow Wilson said, after he had viewed the film, "It was like writing history with lightning."

The movie was about the Civil War and its aftermath, and it was directed by a very Southern gentleman. Griffith was... well, let's not pull punches... Griffith was a bigot and he portrayed African Americans as little more than animals.

To this day, when *The Birth of a Nation* is shown it is picketed by the NAACP.

The heroes of the movie are men in white robes riding horses and wearing Christian crosses... the Ku Klux Klan.

And it wasn't just the cities that the Klan attracted. In New Hampshire, according to the 1955 Charlestown town history, in June of 1924, there was a big Klan gathering out in a natural amphitheater in a field on the McCrea farm in the northern part of town.

People came from all over New England, over five hundred in all. The newspaper reported two hundred cars parked in the field there.

Two hundred automobiles of 1924 vintage or earlier with their headlights aimed at a wooden speaker's dais which had been built in the center of the field. They covered the rostrum with bunting and surrounded it with lots of American flags.

On the hill above the amphitheater were three huge kerosene-soaked wooden crosses. The center cross was over fifty feet high.

Security was tight. Only persons with invitation cards were admitted to the event.

Speakers in white robes with pointy hats harangued the crowd with anti-black, anti-Roman Catholic, and anti-Jewish rhetoric.

The culmination was setting fire to the crosses. All over the area the burning symbols could be seen, and people talked of nothing else for weeks.

But that was that as far as Charlestown was concerned. The organizers went their way, and the Klan never caught on locally.

And as the town history states, "The whole thing passed into legend."

# Cloud Seeding

SCIENTISTS FROM GENERAL Electric came to Concord, New Hampshire, one year to perform an experiment. And it seemed the whole world was watching to see if this experiment would work.

It was cutting-edge technology. In the short term, if it worked, it would save lives and property. In the long term, it had the promise of changing the world.

The year was 1947, the driest year of the twentieth century in New England. All that summer there had been thousands of grass and forest fires. By fall the woods were a tinder box.

Then on October 15, a raging forest fire wiped out a big section of Kennebunkport in Maine.

Two hundred thousand acres were burned; 851 homes and 397 vacation homes were leveled by the fire.

That same day, October 15, there were brush and forest fires in New Hampshire in Laconia, Raymond, Atkinson, Farmington and Sandwich. Homes were destroyed on Province Lake and around Sunapee.

Two days later half the eastern side of Mt. Desert Island in Maine burned; 67 estates on what was called Millionaires' Row were leveled, and five hotels.

It took an entire month to put the fire out and, by that time, 17,000 acres had burned and an additional 170 homes were gone.

Twenty thousand acres burned around Ossipee Mountain and 58 homes in South Waterboro burned.

A week later a disastrous fire happened along the Boston and Maine Railroad in Farmington, New Hampshire.

Now, you probably wonder what this has to do with an experiment done by General Electric. Well, I'm coming to that.

It all has to do with a former Appalachian Mountain Club hut-system guy named Raymond Falkner.

Back in the 1930s, Ray Falkner was right on the cutting edge of weather forecasting. By 1942, he was a weather observer up at the Mt. Washington Observatory. He was doing research on ice buildup on airplane wings and how cold affected synthetic rubber tires.

In 1946 he was hired away by GE in Schenectady, New York. He was hired to do experiments with Nobel Prize winner Irving Langmuir and scientist Vincent Schaefer. Vincent Schaefer was the person who discovered that clouds could be seeded with dry ice or water or iodine crystals and made to give up their water.

So.

On the afternoon of October 29, 1947, a plane took off from Concord Airport and flew over the cumulus clouds northeast of Concord which were over a brushfire in progress.

It was the first practical application of cloud seeding in history.

And what happened?

Well, very little happened. Some reported that a little moisture was generated. But most, that day, saw no precipitation at all.

It was a great idea. And it had to be tried. But it didn't work. And it wasn't tried again.

But on that day, all eyes were on Concord, New Hampshire.

# Reserve the Right to Refuse Service

ONE OF THE saddest facts about out country is how much prejudice there used to be.

When I was in the United States Army back in 1958, black soldiers could not sit and drink coffee in any restaurant in downtown Baltimore.

From the State of Delaware south, there were signs in all the restaurants reading, "We reserve the right to refuse service to anyone."

And before you begin to feel superior for living in the North, let me tell you that virtually all the grand hotels in the White Mountains, save those in Bethlehem, also "reserved the right to refuse service to anyone." That refusal was aimed principally at Jewish clientele. But African Americans and any other persons of dark complexion also were not welcome in the rooms of these "grand" hotels.

Over in Bethlehem, however, many of the hotels were owned by and catered exclusively to Jews.

But Jews were not welcome at the Crawford House or the Profile House or the Wambek... or Wentworth by the Sea down in New Castle, for that matter.

Scuyler Dodge, the former owner of the Mountain View House told me during an interview a few years ago that right up into the 1960s, the hotel had never rented a room to anyone Jewish.

Former hotel owner and historian Ed Brummer, who incidentally is as tolerant and nice a man as I know, tells me that, at the Mt. Washington Hotel back in the thirties, if someone deemed "undesirable" drove past the gate house they would call up to the desk and say that (and this is a quote) "The cows are out."

Of course the hotel would be all booked up and "We are terribly sorry but we seem to have lost your reservation."

# *Lobster Dinner*

THIS STORY TOOK place up on Lake Umbagog in Errol a few years ago.

Seems Dr. Ovide Lamontagne of Manchester had a cottage on the lake, and one weekend in the fall, he had a half-dozen of his buddies up to hunt and tell lies and have a good old testosterone party.

Now there they are on the northernmost shore of Lake Umbagog when someone has the great idea of having a lobster dinner.

It's possible because one of the party was Captain Guy Caron who was a pilot for Northeastern Airlines. And Captain Caron was friends with Dick Pinette, who was a bush pilot and lived over in Berlin.

Well, there was a phone at the camp and so they called Pilot Pinette up and asked if he'd deliver eighteen live lobsters a couple days hence. "Sure," Pilot Pinette said. One problem: Pilot Pinette's plane didn't have pontoons and there was no place to land near the lake. Clearly some expedience was needed, and if there was anything he could do, it was expedite.

So a couple days later, the guys are out at the lakefront when the plane comes over. In the plane are three large burlap bags. In each bag are six live lobsters rolled up in hay. Also in each bag is an empty plastic milk carton so the bags will float in the water.

Brilliant! Except Pilot Pinette looks down to see that overnight the lake has frozen too thick to launch a boat, too thin to walk on.

What to do?

Well, the pilot passes low over the cottage and, bombs away, he drops the sacks on land . . . one at a time and all three sacks land within fifteen feet of the building. Then he makes one more pass and drops a note wishing the guys well with their dinner. The note is attached to a thirty-foot streamer so they can find it. Problem is that the streamer gets caught in a treetop.

A miracle. All the lobsters survived the fall. Just one broken claw.

A beautiful meal was served that night and later they went out to see what was attached to the streamer. They threw rocks and they fired weapons at the message. Nothing would bring it down. Finally a chain saw was used and the message retrieved. And for years that message was displayed on the wall there in the camp.

Ah . . . men and their hunting.

Anybody tells you the good old days were better. Don't you believe it.

# THE TOWNS

## *Barnstead*

THE REV. JOSEPH Adams was U.S. President John Adams' uncle.

The Reverend Adams was for sixty-eight years the minister at the Congregational Church in Newington, New Hampshire. He preached there until the day he died in 1783, at the age of ninety-four.

That church, by the way, still exists. It is, in fact, the oldest meetinghouse in New Hampshire.

President Adams, on occasion, would come up from Quincy to stay with his uncle for a few days and attend services at the church. He said of his uncle that his sermons were "preached in a powerful and musical voice, quoting texts and chapters of the scripture without notes."

Now in 1727, Lieutenant Governor John Wentworth charged Reverend Adams with the job of finding settlers for a tract of land located on the new Province Road near the Suncook River, south of Lake Winnipesaukee.

Reverend Adams proposed resettlement of the area to his parishioners and to friends and college classmates from Harvard.

In the end, people from Newington and from as far away as Long Island and Cape Cod came north to settle the land.

Many on the Cape came from Barnstable and those from New York from Hampstead.

From these two names, Barnstable and Hampstead, which they cobbled together using the first and last syllable of each place, came the name Barnstead. And Barnstead it has been ever since.

Barnstead, by the way, has a total of nine ponds and lakes. When we say "lakes region," this is what we are talking about.

# *Benton*

COVENTRY, CONNECTICUT, IS named for Coventry, England.

Coventry, England, was the place where St. Michael's Church was bombed in World War II.

Winston Churchill knew that the city would be attacked by the Luftwaffe. He knew this because the English had broken the Nazi code. But Churchill sacrificed the city and the cathedral so as not to tip his hand to Germany that the Allies had the code.

All this in passing. It has nothing to do with this place . . . except for the name . . . Coventry.

The Connecticut town may have gotten its name from the English town or from one George William Coventry, Earl of Coventry.

Anyhow, we do know this. Back in 1764, ten years before the American Revolution, a bunch of settlers came from Connecticut, and one of them was a guy named Theophilius Fitch who came from Coventry.

Fitch was a friend of New Hampshire Colonial Governor Wentworth and the nephew of one of the governor's teachers at Harvard.

So the fix was in.

And this town was named Coventry, New Hampshire.

For seventy-five years, Coventry went about its affairs, but prosperity never visited it. The growing season was short on the shoulders of Mt. Moosilauke and, except for a corner of the town, it was bypassed by commerce and industry and the railroad.

Places like Haverhill and Bath regarded their neighbors in Coventry as the ultimate hicks. There were jokes about the backwater people who lived there.

Then came 1839. This was a time when there was great hope in America. It was the time of "Tippecanoe and Tyler, too." Martin van Buren was the Democrat, and he lost to William Henry Harrison. But the loss was not due to the votes in Coventry. The Coventry yokels were Jackson Democrats. They went for Van Buren 73 to 9.

It was about this time that the people in Coventry had just about had it. They were mad as hell and weren't going to take it any more.

As a first step, they decided to change their name.

But to what? Well, the leading Democrat of the day was Senator Thomas Hart Benton of Missouri. He was the natural successor to Van Buren and before him, Jackson.

Seventy-three to nine was the ratio of Democrats in the town and their choice of a new name reflected this. Only two citizens voted against the new name. Those citizens, the town history reports, were Major Samuel Mann and Ira Witcher. The vote was seventy-seven to two . . . an even greater margin than had gone for Van Buren.

And from that time on, this town has been Benton.

By the way, Senator Thomas Hart Benton's daughter was married to the great American explorer and politician, John C. Fremont, for whom the town of Fremont, New Hampshire, was to take its name fifteen years later.

Oh, and also Thomas Hart Benton was not the artist . . . he was, in fact, the uncle of that Thomas Hart Benton.

# Boscawen Native

CAN YOU GUYS guess the name of this person?

His mother was a cousin of the Duke of Marlborough.

His father was the Viscount Falmouth and a cousin of Admiral Edward Vernon, who was the hero of Portobello in the Caribbean in 1739. Admiral Vernon is the man for whom the town of Mont Vernon, New Hampshire, is named.

And he, himself, enlisted at the age of twenty-nine under Admiral Vernon. He spent his life in the British navy and ended up a vice admiral of a squadron. It was under his leadership that the navy captured Louisbourg in Canada, one of the great victories of the wars with France and Spain.

He died in 1761, and one year later the royal governor of New Hampshire named a town for him.

The man is Admiral Edward Boscawen and the town is, of course, Boscawen.

In 1958, I was drafted into the Army and was processed through the fort where most of the soldiers in World War II were processed; that is, Fort Dix. Back then, I had no idea how the fort got its name.

Turns out, it is named for another man born in Boscawen: General John Adams Dix, who was a hero of the Civil War and the highest-ranked volunteer officer in the army. It was General John Adams Dix who suppressed the draft riots in New York City during the war.

His most famous edict was issued when he was made U.S. Secretary of the Treasury at the start of the Civil War. This was his "American Flag Dispatch." In it he said, "If anyone attempts to haul down the American Flag shoot him on the spot!"

General Dix died in New York City in 1879.

Boscawen, by the way, is not pronounced Boscawen by the natives there. The old-timers in town pronounce the name as it was pronounced a hundred years ago. They say "Bosk-wain."

No one seems to know how the man for whom the town is named pronounced his name, but I'll bet it was "Bosk-wain."

## *Bradford*

THEY CALLED THE place New Bradford because the first people to settle there came up from Bradford, Massachusetts.

Later, in 1771 when Colonial Governor John Wentworth granted the incorporation, they adopted the name Bradfordtown.

But sixteen years later they changed the name back to simply, Bradford. And Bradford it has remained ever since.

Some think that the name came from Governor William Bradford of the Pilgrims and Plymouth Plantation, but that is not the case. In fact, the name of the original town in Massachusetts came from the town of Bradford, which is in Yorkshire, England.

Perhaps the most famous person to come from this town was Colonel Thomas Stickney. Colonel Stickney was at the center of crossroads for one of the great events of American history.

See, in 1787 Colonel Stickney was the moderator of the New Hampshire delegation convened in Concord that year to vote either to support or not to support the ratification of the United States Constitution.

Frankly, most of the delegates had been against the country adopting a Constitution. These people were called Anti-Federalists and they wanted a strong state government, not a strong federal government.

The year before, at a meeting in Exeter, those in favor of ratifying the Constitution had seen the writing on the wall and, using a parliamentary trick, managed to postpone a vote until the delegates could reassemble in Concord the next year.

The delegates, under the strong leadership of Colonel Stickney, managed to get enough votes to become the ninth state to ratify the Constitution and, in doing so, provided the two-thirds vote necessary to adopt it.

So it can be said that Colonel Stickney presided over the very moment that we became the United States.

## Number Four Becomes Charlestown

FOR FIFTY YEARS, the place was known as just plain old "Number Four."

That was because it was the fourth settlement and trading post on the Connecticut River coming up from Massachusetts. It was Massachusetts back then.

But then in 1740, his Majesty George II in his wisdom redrew, as it were, the boundaries between Massachusetts and New Hampshire, and a whole bunch of towns found themselves in another state. One of those towns was old "Number Four."

Of course this meant that the charters by which people owned land in those towns were null and void. If pushed, those New Hampshire robber barons could require settlers to pay again for their land . . . or forfeit it. That's why lots of towns wanted to stay with Massachusetts. It was less risky.

Old "Number Four" wanted to stay with Massachusetts.

But Benning Wentworth, New Hampshire's royal governor said, "Nothing doing, you are ours now!"

In the end, the council over in Portsmouth voted to let the people who owned their land under Massachusetts charters transfer those deeds intact to New Hampshire. But they made the populace sweat awhile before they agreed to that.

Anyhow, "Number Four" was now New Hampshire's, and Governor Wentworth saw another chance to toady up to British royalty. See, Benning was friends with Admiral Charles Knowels of the British navy. Charlie was then the Governor of Jamaica. He had a long and distinguished career. During the war with Spain, he fought at Portable and Cartagena with Admiral Edward Vernon, for whom Washington's Mt. Vernon was named, and also the town of Mont Vernon in New Hampshire.

And Admiral Charlie fought at Louisburg, as well. He was a hero. And connected. And Benning Wentworth saw a chance to ingratiate himself with Admiral Charlie by . . . I guess you figured it out . . . by changing good old honest "Number Four" into Charlestown.

One of the original settlers of this town was a blood relative of mine, Efraim Wetherbee, who was a lieutenant in the militia.

The Fort at Number Four played a major part in the French and Indian War, and was as important in the Revolutionary War as a place to put stores and to congregate troops.

The Battles of Saratoga and Ticonderoga and Bennington would probably never have been won were it not for the Fort at Number Four.

Today, of course, the place has been completely recreated in a spot very close to where the original was. Thousands visit it each year.

If you love history or if you have kids or grandchildren it is worth the trip.

# Concord

NOW HOW DID Concord get its name?

By the way, a lot of people don't know it, but Concord used to be way up in the White Mountains. And, "They was robbed," as the saying goes. And I'll tell you about that later.

Most people think the New Hampshire's Concord was named for Concord, Massachusetts. But it wasn't. Concord was, in fact, named the same way the airplane was named . . . the SST, that is.

Here's how it happened.

In the beginning, this section of New Hampshire was named after the Indian tribe who inhabited it. These were the Pennacooks. The area of Concord still called Pennacook is near where the Merrimack and Contoocook rivers join. But all this area was first called "Pennacook." That was back in 1659.

Pennacook, and later a second village downstream, were settled mostly by people from Haverhill, Massachusetts. And those people had come to Haverhill for the most part from Essex in England. In 1733, they incorporated and called this settlement Rumford.

Now down the river was, of course, the town of Bow. And this is where the genesis of Concord's name began. See, Rumford and Bow couldn't agree on where the border was between their towns. There was a lot of fighting, but finally, in 1765, the boundary was agreed upon . . . peacefully as it were.

And in commemoration of this peaceful agreement, the town of Rumford became Concord which is the Latin word for peace. It was a concord, in other words, like the airplane was, a peaceful agreement between England and France. And that, too, is a "Concorde." So there is the airplane connection.

As for the White Mountain connection, in 1765, it seems there was already a Concord, New Hampshire, up there, and the people in this other Concord were told to choose another name.

They chose "Gunthwaite."

Yeah, I never heard of a "Gunthwaite, New Hampshire," either, and that's because the people there didn't take to the new name and soon changed it to . . . right, Lisbon.

In 1800, this Concord replaced Portsmouth as the state's capital.

And there you have it. The name Rumford lives on, of course. Down Maine there is a town named "Rumford Falls." There is the "Rumford Press." And, as you may remember, there is Concord's illustrious early citizen, Benjamin Thompson, who during the Revolution, ran off to Europe . . . invented a number of other things which had to do with cannon and warfare. He was knighted by King George III and also named "Count Rumford" by the Holy Roman Emperor himself.

He is, not incidentally, the man for whom "Rumford Baking Powder" is named.

# Famous from Croydon

CROYDON IS LOCATED north of Newport and south of Grantham on Route 10.

Population, 660. Croydon is a very small town.

It is noted mostly for the Corbin Park, a 25,000-acre game preserve where people hunt for bear and wild boar. Teddy Roosevelt himself hunted there. So did President Herbert Hoover.

Austin Corbin, for whom the park is named, was a nineteenth-century railroad magnate who was born in Croydon. It is a pretty private place. There aren't many stories in the press about Corbin Park.

A couple other famous people came from this town as well: Samuel Reed Hall and Ruel Durkee.

Sam Hall was born there way back in 1795. He graduated from Kimball Academy at Meriden and became a school teacher. It was not a gratifying profession to him, and he had some radical ideas about teaching.

Later he became a Congregational minister in Concord, Vermont. It was in Concord that Professor Hall established a teachers' college.

At the Concord school Professor Hall wrote, "The entire system of education in America is defective and in need of drastic reform." And he set about reforming it.

Many educational historians write that Sam Hall was the first American schoolteacher who used a blackboard.

Kids, of course, back then had individual slates to write on as paper was very expensive. Abe Lincoln, you may recall, used the blade of a shovel and a piece of charcoal because even a slate and chalk were dear on the frontier.

But Professor Hall used a large slate blackboard at the front of the class.

In his life, he was the principal of the teachers' seminary at Phillips Andover Academy in Massachusetts, and later at what is now Plymouth State University in New Hampshire. He wrote many textbooks and before his death was the foremost authority on education in the country.

Now Ruel Durkee was not an educated man but he was highly intelligent. He was a tanner and a landowner in Croydon and, just after the Civil War, he became the most powerful man in the entire state of New Hampshire.

Ruel Durkee was the political boss of the Granite State. He held his power by way of controlling what towns would get railroad lines through them.

The large room on the north side of the first floor of the Eagle Hotel in Concord was where Ruel Durkee did business. Those who voted his way received free railroad passes to travel anywhere in the country.

This was powerful stuff back before there were automobiles and good roads.

Durkee was powerful, I say, but he was not hated. In fact, he was respected.

At the end of his life, he had little money. He had forgiven debts and given most of it away. People loved him for his kindness; although, if you crossed him he could be hard.

In the end his friends raised a monument on his grave in the Croydon Cemetery.

By the way, perhaps one of the most entertaining books ever written about New Hampshire was *Coniston* by Winston Churchill. Not the Winston Churchill of England but America's most popular author at the turn of the twentieth century. "Coniston" is the name given Croydon in this novel, and Ruel Durkee is called Jethro Bass.

The book is a romantic comedy and highly readable. I highly recommend it. Oh, yeah, and you will note that the general store in Croydon is called The Coniston Store.

# Francestown Soapstone

NEW HAMPSHIRE IS called The Granite State because, at one time in this country's history, more granite was quarried in New Hampshire than in any other place in America.

But did you know that, at one time, the finest soapstone in the world also came from New Hampshire?

Well it did, specifically from Francestown.

It began in 1794. A hardscrabble farmer named Daniel Fuller was plowing his field and noticed that his plow did not make a grating noise when it passed over a rock outcropping.

What Daniel Fuller had discovered was a wonderfully pure deposit of steatite. Steatite is soapstone, a rock composed of talc. The rock is soft and can be cut with woodworking tools. It can be carved into mantle pieces and sills; it is a wonderful material for kitchen sinks, and it also holds heat wonderfully.

In 1794 not many things were made of soapstone. But Daniel Fuller was a wily guy. He opened a small quarry and kept its production low. That way, he limited the amount of soapstone on the market and was able to keep his prices high. He died a wealthy man in 1847.

The business then passed to Fuller's son and his wife. At their deaths, the quarry was divided between their son and the son of a friend, one Abner Woodward. No one seems to know why Woodward got this inheritance; it is only recorded that he got it.

Woodward had been a poor man, no assets whatsoever. Overnight the inheritance made him wealthy. Within one year he became the town's leading taxpayer. Soon his partner, Fuller's grandson, was out of the picture.

About this time, the Civil War commenced and demand for soapstone became astronomical. Overnight, it seems, soapstone was all the rage. People loved soapstone stoves because they held the heat so well and radiated it more evenly. The railroads issued heated blocks of soapstone to keep passengers' feet warm. Francestown even provided soapstone for foot warmers for the entire British railroad system.

Two thousand tons of soapstone were taken each year from the quarry. The Francestown Soapstone Stove Company turned out four thousand stoves in 1867 alone.

But after the war Woodward made some bad business decisions. The quarry was 135 feet deep and getting the stone out had become very expensive, and Woodward had not been able to keep his prices high enough to make a profit. In 1882, the business went bankrupt.

New owners were able to keep the business afloat with a much restricted production schedule. In 1912, the company decided to open a new vein of stone across the road from the principal quarry. A dynamite explosion caused a fire, which spread to the entire group of quarry buildings and burned two large private homes to the ground as well. Litigation and payment of damages due to the fire ruined the company. It never recovered.

That's the story of the Francestown soapstone quarry. One of the remarkable things about this story is that the vein of stone is still there. And, yes, over the years there have been a few attempts to resurrect the operation, but none have been successful.

# Garrison Hill

*This tower on Garrison Hill overlooks the city of Dover.*

BACK IN THE late 1880s, Dover had a horse railroad which ran from down by Sawyer's Mills, through the city and toward Dover, a distance of about three miles. This was like a trolley car on tracks except it was pulled by horses. Later it would become an electric trolley line.

Just outside of town there was a rise of land which had been called "The Great Hill of Cocheco," and later on, "Varney's Hill" after the family that owned it. But the family sold the land. And from about 1830 on, it was called "Garrison Hill" after the garrison houses that once surrounded it.

But, like I say, in the 1880s the horse trolley went by the road that led up to the summit of Garrison Hill, so the owners of the railroad decided to build a 65-foot-high wooden tower on the top of the hill with a small restaurant in the base.

From the top of the tower you could see clear to Boston and all the way to Mt. Washington. It cost ten cents to go up the tower and use the telescope there. What this meant was that families would use the horse railroad on the weekends as well as for getting to work during the week.

Later on, they built a roller-skating rink on the hill and a band concert platform. A few years later there were plans for a toboggan slide down the hill.

But in 1897, a careless smoker accidentally set a fire that burned the tower to the ground. And that was that. The recreation area had lasted only seventeen years.

But then in 1911, the widow of a very rich citizen died. Abby Sawyer had remembered the wonderful park and the fun she had had there. Abby bequeathed the town $3,000 to rebuild the tower, this time of steel... and $500 to improve the road leading up to it. The tower was to be dedicated to the memory of her husband, Joseph Sawyer. It wasn't quite enough money to do the job, but the town agreed to shoulder the extra expense. And so, in 1913, this magnificent steel tower opened and it was a huge success. By the 1950s there was skiing and a warming hut and a tow, and people were using the hill year round.

But then it all changed. Some said it was because of television, others thought that the roads had gotten so good, people could get to bigger attractions in very little time. Whatever the reason, by the mid-sixties few people were visiting the old tower.

By the 1970s there had been severe vandalism and the structure was rusting away. The city fenced it off and petitioned the court to change the terms of Abby's will so that the structure could be torn down. In the meantime, the old tower just sat there rusting away.

In the 1980s, a committee tried to find federal money and, about this time, the citizens began to put some real effort into saving the tower. The Boy Scouts cleaned up the park, and the place was accepted on the National Register of Historic Places.

But it was too late. The tower was beyond saving. It was a danger and had to be torn down.

What to do?

Why, rebuild it again using the original plans!

It seemed impossible, but it could be done. The big push came in the 1990s. The whole town pitched in. Virtually all the labor and materials and money came from private sources and from people hell-bent on saving a great landmark.

And rebuilt it was.

On October 16, 1993, the eight-ton copper roof was lifted into place and the Garrison Hill tower again looked to Boston. The entire job had been done for $60,000. Donations of labor and services were estimated to be around $300,000.

And the town of Dover got its landmark back . . . and its pride.

## Ghost Hollow

QUITE A FEW years back, there was a guy who kept the general store up at Groggy Harbor, about a half a mile north of Campton. Guy's name was George Ward.

Now George, he was a practical joker and was forever playing tricks on his customers, like putting a couple bricks in the bottom of the paper bag that a customer had to carry, so that when they got home all sweaty they'd know that it wasn't the weight of the Post Toasties that brought on their massive coronary.

George Ward lived on the road that goes through the ravine on the way to North Woodstock. And one day he went out and nailed a big plank right on to the top of the fence posts there where the road was about to make a curve.

Then he waited 'til after sunset. Soon an unsuspecting soul came by on their way home.

George then threw a white bed sheet over himself so he looked like a ghost and mounted the board. In the darkness he appeared to be floating above the fence making all sorts of hooting noises.

Dozens of people were scared out of their wits, and George was having a gay old time 'til one night when a guy named Tom Welch was walking through the hollow. George mounted the plank.

"OOOOOO . . . OOOOOhh," he said.

"OOO yourself, you jerk," Tom Welch said and tore a stake out of the fence and attacked the ghost.

George Ward in a sheet, pursued by Tom Welch with a stick; it was a lovely sight.

Tom caught him, and the ghost began to wail in earnest.

Needless to say, George Ward never did that prank again.

But, you know, to this day that spot in the woods is called "Ghost Hollow."

# *Gilford*

ON THE IDES of March, during the American Revolution in 1781, British General Charles Cornwallis came up against American troops under the command of General Nathaniel Green in a little backwater place in North Carolina called the Guilford Courthouse.

The British won that battle, but it was a Pyrrhic victory. They suffered many more casualties than did the Patriot troops that day. A quarter of Cornwallis' men were put out of action in the battle. General Cornwallis was so disheartened by the battle that he abandoned the far south and marched his men to Virginia.

So historians see this as a turning point in the war...a place where the Americans showed their mettle.

At that battle that day was a sergeant from Newington, one Lemuel Mason. For the rest of his life, Lemuel Mason dined out on his stories about that battle.

Later when he came back, he moved to the east shore of Winnipesaukee Lake in a place called the Gunstock Parish, so-called because it was located in the shadow of Gunstock Mountain.

Gunstock Mountain was called so, not because the range of hills is in the shape of a gunstock, as many think, but rather because legend has it an unnamed settler broke the stock of his gun while hunting there.

Anyhow, Lemuel Mason was one of the founders of a new town there which he named after his favorite subject. The town is, of course, Gilford. That makes Gilford the only town in the state to take its name from a battle site of the Revolutionary War.

That site, Guilford Courthouse, took its name from one Frederick Lord North who was prime minister of England and (and here it is) the Earl of Guildford, which is spelled G-U-I-L-D FORD. But the "D" was never pronounced. In England, it was always "gill ford." (And a note here; the town of Guildhall, Vermont, also had a "D" in its name but is pronounced "gill hall."

The practical New Hampshire people just left the "D" off. Of course, that doesn't explain the "U" in G-U-I-L FORD.

By the way, after the battle of Guilford Courthouse the people down there in North Carolina changed the name of the place to Martinsville.

## Goshen

IN THE MIDDLE of the eighteenth century, much of the land around Sunapee was called Saville.

The three original families who settled there were the Grindells, the Rands and the Langs.

Settler Daniel Grindell was a relative of Edmund Grindell, Archbishop of Canterbury. Benjamin Rand was a cousin of New Hampshire Colonial Governor John Wentworth. And Benjamin Rand's sister Elizabeth was married to the third member of this original settling triumvirate, William Lang.

Rand's Pond in this town is named, by the way, for Benjamin Rand.

All three of these original settlers had served in the French and Indian Wars and had received their grants there from Thomas Martyn of Portsmouth. Martyn was "Keeper of Military Stores" under General Amherst in the war with the French.

Later on, one of the triumvirates, Daniel Grindell, would go on to serve as a captain in the Revolutionary War, serving under General George Washington himself.

After the Revolutionary War, a lot of soldiers who served under Washington settled there. By that time, the area was made up of some five different towns: Lempster, Unity, Newport, Sunapee, and Newbury.

By 1791, a community had grown up, and at that time the citizens petitioned the governor of the state, Josiah Bartlett, to make this area into their own town.

Their request was granted and they chose the name Goshen because most of the men who settled there had fought in the Revolutionary War in a regiment composed of soldiers from the town of Goshen, Connecticut.

And Goshen it remains.

# Grafton

BEFORE THE CIVIL WAR, there were very few morticians in the country towns of America. But the war produced a spate of them. Soldiers who died in the war had to be embalmed in order to be sent home on the railroads.

So there was an industry that grew with the war as more and more people learned embalming.

Before the war, families would wash and arrange their loved one, and the funeral would take place in a day or so . . . or sooner if it was summertime.

But the war produced a lot of morticians and, after the war, they went home and opened businesses.

Often they would come to the home of the family and do their work there.

Places like Grafton were way out in the pucker bush, as it were, and it was pretty late before high-falutin funerals came hereabouts. And when change did come, it came in the form of a town hearse. It arrived by railroad in 1883: a beautiful black hearse to be pulled by two black horses and driven by a teamster.

The hearse was the property of the town of Grafton and was handmade by the George Russell and Sons Company and cost $250 plus $20.88 for the Northern Railroad delivery.

The next year the town also purchased snow runners for wintertime trips to the graveyard.

The old tramp house by the railroad tracks was expanded to house the vehicle and anyone could avail themselves of its use for the cost of the services of the teamster.

People in Grafton were proud of their horse-drawn hearse and it was used for thirty years . . . up until the coming of paved roads and automobiles in the 1920s.

The last time it was used was 1924. By that time, there were funeral parlors over in Bristol and Lebanon, and few wanted the horses for their last ride . . . all except Burt Heath. Burt was a Grafton resident who could not abide the newfangled gasoline-powered hearses, and he vowed never to ride in one.

The kids in town knew of his wishes and every Halloween, it seems, they would break into the hearse house and steal the wagon and park it in Burt's driveway.

The town had the hearse until 1949 and used it only for parades and to show as a curiosity. That year they sold it to an antique dealer.

Heaven knows where it is today.

And Burt . . . Burt never did get to ride in it . . . formally.

# Grantham

THOMAS ROBINSON WAS an English peer. He was a graduate of Trinity College, Cambridge, and a man to be reckoned with. In the 1700s he served as Minister to Paris under England's first prime minister, Sir Robert Walpole.

Sir Bobby, by the way, is the man for whom Walpole, New Hampshire, was named.

Sir Thomas Robinson was on the fast track, as I say, and he came back to England and became one of the country's first postmasters general.

Charles III bestowed Sir Tommy with the title of Lord Grantham.

So I guess you have guessed it. When this town was chartered in 1761, New Hampshire Governor Benning Wentworth, in his rush to toady up to the rich and famous of the time, named the place Grantham.

And so it has been called ever since.

Governor Wentworth, had he been alive at the time, would have rued his decision to call a New Hampshire town Grantham; for, it turned out, Lord Grantham was one of the champions of American Independence back in jolly old England.

He is quoted as saying that the Americans would certainly "fight for their own altars and firesides."

Grantham is the town where the community of Eastman is located.

And for years, Grantham was noted for a guy named Lemuel Cooper who raised a hog that weighed 1,000 pounds. The swine was so celebrated that after it was slaughtered Cooper had the skin stuffed and it was exhibited at the 1876 Centennial World's Fair in Philadelphia.

# Hampton Falls

ON THE LAST Sunday of October back in 1727, the Rev. Mr. Goodkin, pastor of the Hampton Falls Church, preached a sermon entitled "The Day of Trouble Is Near."

The next day a terrible earthquake struck the town. Written descriptions of that earthquake are in the Hampton Falls town history.

The day was bright and sunny. The night before there had been a full moon and not a cloud in the sky. But then after noon it commenced.

First there was a terrible noise ... something, the history tells us, like thunder. Houses trembled as if falling down. Tops of chimneys fell, and people on Morton Hill observed the earth to open and blue flames to run on about the earth.

People all over town saw flashes of light. The sea roared in an unusual manner. Places that had been solid ground became swampy. Natural springs disappeared, only to reappear in different places.

Brute creatures, the history tells us, (that is cows and oxen and sheep) ran about the fields as in the greatest distress. For days afterwards there were aftershocks.

Then again, less than two months later, on Christmas Eve, there was another quake. This one was not nearly as violent as the first; but it was strong enough to be felt from Boston to Casco Bay.

Enough to send people back to church.

And for days after the quake around Morton Hill, there was the smell of sulfur. A smell so strong it changed the name of the place.

To this day, it is known as "Brimstone Hill."

# Harrisville

I'VE SAID THIS before, and it's true, so I'm saying it again. Some of the prettiest towns in New Hampshire begin with the letter "h."

Hopkinton, Hillsboro Center, Hancock, Haverhill, Hanover, Hampstead, and the town which is unique in all of New England: Harrisville.

People were there as early as 1760, although then the place was part of a number of other towns . . . Hancock, Dublin, Roxbury, Nelson, Marlboro.

But, you see, they had terrific water power. A little dam and an immediate drop of a couple hundred feet made it a natural for a mill.

Sure enough, a mill was built there. First there was a blacksmith shop, though. A guy named Jason Harris operated it. He was succeeded by Erasmus Harris, who built the first mill. Erasmus' son, Bethuel, expanded it, and his son, Milan, expanded it again.

By the mid-nineteenth century this was one of the thriving woolen centers of the country and one of the first. The first in the state, of course, was over in Highbridge in New Ipswich.

When the mills were at their peak, this place was known as Twitchellville after an early settler named Abel Twitchell. Abel had a daughter, Deborah, and she married Bethuel Harris.

The mills needed workers and foremen and executives, and soon the town looked as it does today . . . almost entirely built of brick.

Later the Harris Mills were incorporated under the name Cheshire Mills. At that time, (that time being 1870), Milan Harris suggested that the town itself incorporate under the name of Harris.

And so it was, and is, Harrisville.

Milan Harris, by the way, also had a second town named after him. No doubt you have guessed what town that is . . . right, Milan, up in Coos County.

Today Harrisville remains almost as it was in the mid-eighteen hundreds. It is, in fact, the finest preserved example of a New England mill town in the entire country.

# Hebron

IN 1761, CHARLES Wyndham, Earl of Egremont, succeeded William Pitt as British Secretary of State. Like Pitt, Lord Egremont was a fan of the English Colonies in America, and he favored being lenient with us in matters of taxation. That, of course, made him very popular over here.

He was a cousin of New Hampshire Colonial Governor Benning Wentworth and Benning, as he did to a hundred other friends and relatives, decided to name a town for him. In fact, he named two towns for Charles Wyndham. The first was Windham.

But Charles Wyndham, Earl of Egremont, was also Baron Cockermouth. In 1761, the year Wyndham became secretary of state, Benning Wentworth chose a place in the middle of the state and named it Cockermouth. And Cockermouth it remained until 1792.

That's the year Cockermouth was divided into two towns . . . Groton and Hebron.

Now Hebron is the name of an Old Testament city in Palestine or Israel on the West Bank.

Naming a town after a biblical place is quite common even here in the Granite State. The town of Canaan, New Hampshire, also takes its name from the Old Testament, as does Goshen.

One of the early settlers of Hebron was Samuel Phelps. Phelps is an old and illustrious New England family. Alexander Phelps was one of the founders of Dartmouth College. He, in fact, married Dr. Eleazer Wheelock's daughter. Wheelock was, of course, the first president of Dartmouth.

Anyhow all the Phelps family, including Samuel, came from Hebron, Connecticut, and so when the town was split off from what would become Groton, it was Phelps who convinced the townsfolk to adopt the name of his former home. So, in 1792, this place became Hebron.

Somehow I have the feeling that the name Cockermouth wouldn't have lasted anyway.

However, the river in town remains the same. It is still called the Cockermouth River.

# Hooksett

IT WAS FIRST called "Chester Woods" and later "Rowe's Corner." But sometime around the Revolutionary War, folks began to call this place, this place where the Merrimack River swings back upon itself, "Hooksett."

The name wasn't officially adopted until 1822. Everyone seemed to like the name, but to this day, no one seems to know where it came from. There are guesses though.

Some think it is because the river hooks around the big outcropping called the Pinnacle. Much as Bow got its name because the river bowed in that place. On some maps the Pinnacle is called a French name, the "Isle du Hooksett."

Some documents refer to the place as "Ana-hooksett" or "Ama-hookset" or "Onna-hookset" which may, or may not, indicate Native American origin.

Some think that Hooksett takes its name from the lower falls, called "Hookline Falls" by some, because of the great number of fish that, at one time, were caught there . . . shad and eels and salmon and sturgeon.

Charles Hardey in his book, *Hooksett Historical Sketches*, imagines the name was a combination of two locations on the rapids where early people used to fish.

There was the "setting place" where one might set a net, and "hooking place" where one might fish with a line.

Voila: "hook-set."

Mmmmn . . . nahh.

# *Legend of Granite Lake*

USED TO BE that when you went to Keene from Hillsboro or Antrim or Hancock, you would go by Granite Lake in Monsonville, which is a part of Stoddard.

The old Route 123 just skirted the south shore of the lake.

When the bypass was built a dozen years ago or so, the lake settled back into relative anonymity.

But I always found the place quite mystical.

There is, in fact, a legend about Granite Lake.

The story takes place way back during the French and Indian Wars.

There is an island in the middle of Granite Lake. It is called by some "Mileto."

Because it is so large in comparison to the lake, this island seems like a piece of art surrounded by a water frame.

Now on this island there lived an old Native American chief, Chief Pokahoket.

With the old brave was his daughter, Mamowich.

Mamowich was proud of her father. In years past, he had been an important person. Many had come to him for advice. And, in fact, many still made the trip to visit the old man when they needed guidance.

For many years Mamowich tended her father without complaint.

Then one day a young white man came to the island.

The man was gentle and spoke French. Unlike the English speakers, he had tact and confidence and charm. The tribes in New England trusted the French.

And so it was on the island.

The young man was reconnoitering and surveying the area. He espied the campfire on the island and waded out to investigate.

There he found the old man and his daughter. Because Pokahoket was old and infirm and could no longer hunt, the pair had been living on fish they caught in the lake. The young visitor brought them venison. And they feasted.

Because it was in a good location, the young man used the island for his base of operations for the entire summer.

No doubt you have guessed what happened. Yes, the young maiden fell in love with the young man and one night told him of her feelings.

Alas, it was not to be. For her love was unrequited. He did not love her.

Embarrassed, she stole away and climbed to the top of a cliff on the island. There she flung herself into the black water.

The young man quickly ran to the spot.

But the maiden did not surface.

The young Frenchman left, broken hearted.

The old chief did not last the winter.

Today it is said that whenever there is a cry of a loon on Granite Lake, it is the spirit of Mamowich calling out her love.

# Newington

NEWINGTON IS A place of contrasts. One third of it is the Pease Tradeport and Airport, the second third of it is composed of commercial development and shopping centers, and the final third is a lovely old Colonial town.

Since the first settlers came to New Hampshire, this place has been a place where differences abutted and sometimes clashed.

The original name of Newington was, in fact, "Bloody Point," and the reason for the name had to do with the original grants given the first settlers by the English crown.

We do not know to this day which town was settled first . . . Portsmouth or Dover. In early 1623, a man named David Thompson settled on Great Bay. He only stayed about a year and then moved to an island in Boston Harbor, which still retains his name.

Now a couple months after Thompson came, another bunch of settlers landed at what is now Dover Neck and set up a settlement there. It was called the Piscataway Plantation.

All the settlements were called "plantations" back then . . . Jamestown Plantation . . .

Plymouth Plantation . . . you get the point.

It would be fifty years before the name New Hampshire would be used for this place, by the way. This was then all a part of Massachusetts.

Anyhow, in the group of new settlers there was a man named Edward Hilton who took over the patent for the land from David Thompson. This land grant was called the Upper Plantation and included Dover Neck and the opposite shore in what is now Newington.

Now at the same time, down the river at what was called the Lower Plantation at Strawbery Banke, they also got a grant . . . which included in its survey all of what is now Portsmouth and all of what is now Newington. Yeah, you guessed it, the Strawbery Banke's grant also included the land on the river that Eddie Hilton and his group claimed.

So early on, they were always fighting over this land.

In 1631, Captain Thomas Wiggin was the acting governor for the Hilton interests at Dover Neck, and Captain Walter Neal was the steward for the Lower Plantation.

One day Captain Wiggin called out Captain Neal, challenging him to a duel with swords there on the shore. The men met and, after some grumbling and a lot of "Sir, you are a cad!" both men calmed down (some say backed down), and the matter wouldn't be settled for another twenty years when the Massachusetts Legislature gave the property to Strawbery Banke.

But who says the old Yankees didn't have a sense of humor? For the next sixty years, from the time of the duel that never happened until Newington became a town in 1713, this was always called, ironically, "Bloody Point."

# Newington Meetinghouse

THIS IS A quiz. Where is the oldest meetinghouse in New Hampshire?

If you guessed Sandown, as I did, you're wrong. Sandown is the most authentic and, perhaps, most beautiful meetinghouse, and it is, certainly, the best restored, but it ain't the oldest.

Sandown's meetinghouse was built in 1774. The Jaffrey Center Meetinghouse dates from the same time, 1774. North Danville's dates from 1760. But the oldest meetinghouse in New Hampshire is the Congregational church in Newington. It was built in 1712, and a church service has been held in the building every Sunday for 290 years!

Unlike Sandown or North Danville, the Newington Meetinghouse does not have its original look. Like many lovely old churches, this one was remodeled in the 1830s. The single spire was replaced with a squared-off design, and the interior was modernized, but the structure is the same and its position beside the graveyard is stunning.

Directly in front of the Newington church sits a curiosity: the town horse block. It was dragged there by oxen in 1713; the year after the church was completed. Early parishioners mounted their horses from this stone.

The parish house for the church also exists just up the street. The restored building dates from 1699, making it one of the oldest in the state.

Behind the meetinghouse are the huge horse stalls. Beside the church sits the Langdon Library and beside the library, the town forest. The town forest is 112 acres in three tracts and has immense historical significance. This is the oldest town forest in the entire United States. It dates from 1710. Wood from these trees was used for the construction of the original town buildings. The trees themselves have not been used in public buildings for years, but profits from the sale of the lumber still goes to the town.

When Pease Air Force Base was built back in 1954, the center of the town became a cul-de-sac right up against the airport. People could no longer come through the town on their way to Greenland.

This isolation stopped growth, but has turned out to be a blessing; for to visit Newington today is to step back in time. It is an experience like going to a museum only better, better because, unlike a museum, there is real life there, in fact, a sense of vitality even. The beautiful old stone elementary school is now used for recreation and is full of kids in the summer, and there is a playground out behind the 1872 brick town hall.

Oh, one other thing, to get to Newington, take your first right off Route 16, just over the Dover Point Bridge going toward Portsmouth. It's a great place, and it is worth a visit.

# Pembroke

ONE PART OF the French and Indian Wars was called Lovewell's War.

It was called "Lovewells War" after Captain John Lovewell. Lovewell was the person who erected a stockade on Ossipee Lake to protect the settlers in the southern part of the state from attack from the Abenaki Indians. And, in 1725, Captain Lovewell led an expedition into what is now Maine to subdue the tribes there. He encountered the enemy at Fryeburg and was killed.

Many of the members of the militia who fought in the French and Indian Wars were paid for their service with land. The provincial government, in fact, gave Lovewell's men land grants in the area. They named this place Lovewellstown.

But then the Masonian grantees and others began carving up the state in other ways, and soon the area was renamed for the river that flows through it. They renamed the place Suncook.

And Suncook it stayed for a few years. But the Suncook area was huge, and soon it was called for the road it was on which was Buckstreet. But in 1759, the citizens of Buckstreet petitioned Portsmouth to become a town, and Governor Benning Wentworth decided to name the place after Henry Herbert, who had married the governor's cousin.

Henry Herbert was the Earl of Pembroke, and Pembroke it has been ever since.

Lord Pembroke, by the way, became England's Lord Chief Justice, and his home was Wilton House. Many think that is where Wilton gets its name.

Lord Pembroke also designed Westminster Bridge in London. And Pembroke in England is also the place where the Lord's home is.

A couple other things: First, Pembroke is spelled PEMBROKE, which should be pronounced "Pembroke" not "Pembrook." Why is it pronounced that way? 'Cause that's how they pronounce it in England.

And secondly, Suncook which is a part of Pembroke, is bigger than the town that contains it. Go figure.

So, over the years, Pembroke has had four different names.

# Peterborough

WHERE DID THE town of Peterborough get its name?

The answer is: we don't know.

Peterborough was either named for a man named Prescott or for a man named Mordant.

See, the first time that the name "Peterborough" appears written down is on a surveyor's description done in 1739. That was less than a year after the area was awarded to a bunch of land speculators from Massachusetts. By the way, at this time New Hampshire was a province of Massachusetts, and our governor was Massachusetts' Jonathan Belcher. He's the one who awarded the land to the speculators. Those included Jeremiah Gridley, John Hill and John Fowle.

The clerk of those proprietors, that is, the "speculators," was one Peter Prescott of Concord, Massachusetts. He drew two lots in this community, so many think he named the place after himself. Lemuel Shattuck's *History of Concord* states that the town was named for Peter Prescott.

But Governor Belcher was friends with the writers Swift, Pope and Locke and, one of the most popular men of the day, a guy named Charles Mordant, who was an English admiral. He was also First Lord of the Treasury under William III. Admiral Mordant was the Earl of Peterborough, ergo the name with a much fancier origin. That is the more generally accepted origin for the town's moniker.

Peterborough historian George Abbott Morrison is of the opinion that the town is named for the Earl of Peterborough but, nevertheless, in his 1954 town history, he says, "We will never be certain."

Some people are of the opinion that Peterborough was named for St. Petersburg in Russia.

## Theater in Portsmouth

PORTSMOUTH HAS HAD a lot of live theater. There is the Seacoast Repertory Theater and the Pontime Theater and the Players Ring and the Music Hall and, in the summer, the Theater in the Park.

The first theatrical company in Portsmouth was formed in the 1790s in a theater which, like the Seacoast Repertory, was on Bow Street. The theater was on the right side of the street just beyond where the rear of the post office is nowadays. It burned in the great fire of 1806, a fire that also consumed all the warehouses in the area and also the Episcopal Church.

But up to that time there was, on occasion, live theater in Portsmouth, albeit amateur theater.

Charles Brewster in his *Rambles about Portsmouth* identifies the actors as young men from some of the prominent families in town. Names like: E. Saint Loe Livermore (now is that a theatrical name, or what?) and Charles Cutts, Samuel Elliot, George W. Prescott and George Long.

All were educated men and all literary men and all between the ages of twenty and twenty-five (which means, I guess, unmarried).

The company built their own scenery and made their own costumes. Shakespeare was extremely popular and like true Elizabethan drama, there were no women on stage but rather delicate young men who would take the female roles.

According to Brewster, the audiences of the time were well pleased with the performances.

For myself, the next time I attend a performance at the Seacoast Repertory in that ultra-modern hall, I intend to think back on where it all started . . . just up the street.

With East Saint Loe Livermore playing Cordelia.

## Sharon First Vote

*In 1940, the voters who walked through the doors of the old schoolhouse in Sharon were in the national spotlight.*

THE FIRST PRIMARY voting returns in the nation come from New Hampshire; specifically, Dixville Notch, where the count is done at the Balsams Hotel just seconds after midnight.

Each primary the national and international press crowd into the ballot room for the announcement of the first votes counted.

Before Dixville Notch, the first primary count used to come from Hart's Location, also up in the White Mountains.

That's the primary election.

But did you know that there was a time when the first completely tabulated returns of the general election were also reported from New Hampshire?

Well, it's true, and that time was the election of 1940.

And the place was Sharon, New Hampshire. Just seconds after midnight on the morning of November 5, 1940, the old brick schoolhouse in Sharon was crowded with reporters from all the national news services. *The New York Times* was there, and radio broadcasters from the Mutual Network and NBC were there. Flash bulbs popped, and there were interviews with virtually the entire franchised population of the town ... all thirty-one voters.

Wendell Wilkie, the Barefoot Boy from Wall Street, was running against Franklin Delano Roosevelt for president of the United States.

The vote was counted and immediately reported coast to coast over the special phone lines set up into the school. Listeners from New York to Los Angeles and Chicago to New Orleans got the news of the first votes cast in America.

And how prophetic was the vote that night? Well ... not very. Sharon went for Wilkie, twenty-four votes; for Roosevelt, seven.

The vote didn't go into the record books, but it did put Sharon, New Hampshire, on the map. At least for a while.

# *Squog*

BEDFORD USED TO be a good deal bigger than it is nowadays. Take for instance, Squog.

Squog used to be a part of Bedford, and for about fifty years it was the part of Bedford that brought in the most money.

Squog, by the way, is the name most people gave to the village of Piscataquog, which was right there where the Piscataquog River and the Merrimack River meet.

This is not to be confused with the Piscataqua River which separated Portsmouth from Kittery, Maine. This similarity in names may have had some part in people calling it simply the "Squog."

The village of Squog occupied an area that went from about where Sullie's Market was to a bit above the Granite Bridge on Manchester's West Side.

Squog was an important place in the early nineteenth century and before because many of the great mast trees were floated down the Piscataquog to the Merrimack, and this is where they were tagged and counted and taxed.

It is also the place you got across the river. In fact, both rivers. There was a ferry there back before they built the Granite Street Bridge. And there was a bridge across the Squog, just down from one of the first mills built around there.

Because of its importance, there were inns and taverns around the rivers.

When the Middlesex Canal was built in Massachusetts, they started on a canal around Manchester and many of the canal men and the builders of the canal lived in Squog because it was right across the river from the entrance to the Amoskeag Canal.

When they built the Granite Street Bridge in 1840, and a little before that, the railroad bridge just downstream, the money was just rolling in, and the citizens of Squog decided their interests lay, not with rural Bedford, but with cosmopolitan Manchester.

And, in 1853, some citizens of Squog petitioned the state legislature to become a part of Manchester. At the same time parts of Goffstown were also to be annexed.

Manchester at that time had about fourteen thousand people. Goffstown had about 2,300 and Bedford, less than 2,000 people.

The people in Bedford didn't want to lose this important part of their town, but the fix was in and they lost.

And Squog went to Manchester.

# *Swanzey Postal Rates*

BACK IN THE early nineteenth century, the United States Postal Service was not as it is today. Back then, if you sent a letter, the further it had to be carried, the more it cost you.

In one of the histories of Swanzey, I found a listing of the rates charged for carrying letters in the United States between 1816 and 1845.

Back then, stamps cost six cents, ten cents, twelve and one-half cents, eighteen and three-quarters cents and twenty-five cents. The twenty-five cent rate was for letters sent to places over 400 miles away.

I am not sure how one paid for an eighteen and three-quarter cent stamp. I knew there were ha' pennies back then but apparently there were quarter pennies, too.

Now, you figure in the nineteenth century most families lived on less than $200 a year. Some farm families operated on practically no cash at all . . . just enough for pins and needles and salt and sugar. Often a family got by on less than $100 a year.

A twenty-five cent stamp back then was about forty bucks in today's money, to get a letter to, say, Washington, D.C.

The history says that earlier it cost $2.74 to send a half-ounce letter from Boston to San Francisco. That's over 400 bucks in today's currency.

But in 1845, the postal service standardized letter-carrying costs. From then on, people paid five cents to send a letter anywhere up to 300 miles away and ten cents for any letter going further than 300 miles.

This change to the lower rates was caused by the coming of the railroad. Prior to that, all mail went by horseback or stage and by sailing ship for further distances. Often it took months for a letter to arrive. But like everything else sold in America, the railroad brought it to you cheaper and faster.

Today, of course, most mail travels by jet.

# Temple

THE TOWN OF Temple is a pastiche of a number of other towns. It is made up of land that once belonged to Wilton, Lyndeborough, New Ipswich and what was called the Peterborough Slip.

Back in the mid-1700s, the people who lived there wanted to petition the governor to become their own town, but the citizens of Wilton were against it. Wilton got most of the taxes from that place. If another town were made there, Wilton would lose a lot of land.

So a watch was set on the citizens to make sure no one went to Portsmouth to petition the colonial governor. Whoever was to try to get to Portsmouth would have to go through Wilton, and Wilton was ready to stop 'em.

Now, the most-noted citizen of the place at the time was General Francis Blood. He had been a representative of the New Hampshire General Court, and he had been a state senator.

It was General Blood who was chosen for the job of getting the incorporation papers through to Governor John Wentworth. General Blood lived in what is now the center of Temple.

Word got out, however, that someone was going to try to get through, and men were posted at all the roads out of town.

But General Blood was a clever guy. He was friendly with Colonel Ezra Towne of New Ipswich, and so he stopped to ask if he might borrow the colonel's clothes, wig and horse. The colonel loved the idea and giggled the whole time General Blood got into the get-up.

The upshot was that General Blood got away with the ruse and, dressed as Colonel Towne, got through the checkpoints with no trouble at all. In two days, he returned with a new town charter.

And Temple became a town.

# Usquebaugh

IF YOU HAVE looked at a map of Manchester, no doubt you have noticed that most of the streets are parallel to one another or at right angles... save for the section up near Manchester Central High School.

This section is called Janesville, and it is among the earliest parts of the Queen City.

Manchester is mostly laid out on a grid because of the Amoskeag Corporation. The mills owned the city for a hundred years and owned much of the real estate, and what they didn't own, they waited for and bought up.

Only mill personnel lived on the neat streets. The messy streets were from the earlier days of the town of Manchester and before that of Derryfield. These messy parts of town were mostly named after families who owned the land. They housed people who could not afford to live in the fancy parts of town.

There was Youngsville out on Candia Road, and Towlesville which was in the area between today's Manchester Street and The Verizon Arena. Later, Towlesville would be taken over by the mill and the streets paralleled up there.

But the only unplanned street section that remains today in Manchester is Janesville. This part of town was named for Jane Young.

Perhaps the most important thing to come out of Janesville is "Usquebaugh." That's spelled U S Q U E B A U G H.

Usquebaugh was made in the basement of a tenement located on the corner of High and Old Wilson Road. The place was owned by the Bartlett family.

But in 1860, a man named Patrick Swiney moved a still into the basement and turned out what he called "medicinal whiskey." He called it "Usquebaugh."

It was prescribed by doctors to patients in need of a stimulant, and dozens of doctors endorsed the product as being of the highest quality.

The whiskey was made entirely of barley and was, we understand, very smooth. Old Swiney also had a snuff grinder and sold that product as well.

In Manchester, Doctor W. W. Brown and Doctor William Bick and Doctor G. H. Hubbard endorsed the product. All were highly regarded.

And Doctor Josiah Crosby wrote:

> I will add that I had a bottle analyzed by one of the best chemists in the country, who pronounced it fine and pure as a spirit, and containing fifteen percent of strength and body over the generality of spirits.

On Patrick Swiney's death the business went to his clerk, a man named Dennis O'Leary. When O'Leary retired in the 1880s, no more "Usquebaugh" was distilled.

# Vermont Secession

A FEW YEARS ago, the citizens of Killington, Vermont, in their wisdom, voted to secede from the Green Mountain State and become a town in the Granite State.

The reason for the secession was, as usual, taxes. Killington liked the "Live Free or Die" spirit and felt they were being taxed to death by Governor Howard Dean's administration. Of course, the vote meant nothing. Aside from the fact that Killington didn't share a border with New Hampshire, there were constitutional issues that could not be overcome.

But we in New Hampshire were feeling quite smug nonetheless. Imagine seceding from your own state!

Well, I don't know if you ever heard of this, but not just one, but a full thirty-four New Hampshire towns once seceded from New Hampshire and joined Vermont. The towns were what are today: Hinsdale, Charlestown, Claremont, Plainfield, Grafton, Lyme, Lisbon, Surry, Acworth, Newport, Grantham, Hanover, Dorchester, Lancaster, Gilsum, Lempster, Cornish, Marlow, Hanover, Haverhill, Piermont, Alstead, Lebanon, Richmond, Westmoreland, Sunapee, Cardigan, Lyman, Bath, Croydon, Landaff, Lincoln, Franconia and Chesterfield. Two-thirds of the citizens of every one of these towns voted to become part of Vermont. Imagine Claremont, Vermont... or Franconia, Vermont.

All this happened back between 1777 and 1781, when George Washington was president of this new republic. And the secession almost succeeded... and, as a result, there was almost a Civil War between New Hampshire and Vermont.

The reason that all the towns out in the western part of the state wanted out of the Granite State was, as usual, taxes.

The towns paid taxes to the state but got almost no services from the state. Roads were terrible back then, and all these towns sent their goods down the Connecticut River... and brought their goods back from places down the river.

So when Vermont petitioned to become their own state, the people in the towns over here said "Count us in too!"

I mean, it would take you a week to get to Exeter; but Windsor, Vermont, was just up (or down) the river. People over here had a lot more in common.

Now the Granite State government, at that time, claimed Vermont as part of New Hampshire. Hadn't Colonial Governor Benning Wentworth chartered the towns here and named them, too? Bennington is, in fact, named for Benning himself. But New York also claimed Vermont as part of its territory . . . granted to them back in the 1600s by Charles II.

But the Vermonters said, "A plague on both your houses. We want to be our own place."

Well, here is how it finally shook out. The problem went to the U.S. Congress and the president to be arbitrated. George Washington wrote the Vermont governor and said that they could be their own state, but only if they quit the annexation of the thirty-three New Hampshire towns and accept the western bank of the Connecticut as the boundary.

But all these New Hampshire towns had been very happy as Vermont towns. They had elected representatives to the Vermont legislature. They had accepted the law enforcement of Vermont.

In fact, a couple guys, John Grandy and Samuel Davis, had refused to recognize the legitimacy of the local constable because he was granted his power from Vermont. As a result the men were imprisoned in the jail at Charlestown.

The upshot was that the New Hampshire Legislature in Exeter voted to raise an army of one thousand men to go to war with Vermont should it become necessary.

But, like I say, Vermont took George Washington's order and became its own state.

And the thirty-three towns reverted back to New Hampshire.

# *Warner*

THERE'S AN OLD Yankee saying, "Oh, Jeez!"

When a Yankee says, "Oh, Jeez," he or she means that a mess has been made; usually a mess that will be near to impossible to clean up.

Such a mess happened in Warner back just after the American Revolution. It was then that the town decided that their meetinghouse was too small and they needed to build a bigger one.

The problem was that the old meetinghouse was on the south side of the Warner River. This was a problem because, since the first meetinghouse had been built, most of the town had grown on the north side of the river.

As the Yankees say, "Oh, Jeez."

Now this was in the 1780s, which is before the Religious Toleration Act was passed. That meant that the construction of the meetinghouse and the salary of the settled minister were paid for out of town taxes.

So the matter had to be worked out at town meeting. Trouble was, half the folks wanted the meetinghouse in the new place and half wanted it rebuilt where it was. One vote went one way and a second vote went the other. There was no way the townspeople were about to solve the problem. That is until they decided on that old Yankee expedient, "Let George do it."

So at the town meeting in the spring of 1788, the good folks of Warner voted to turn the matter over to the state, and let it decide. The selectmen traveled to Concord and petitioned the general court for a solution. And the general court, in its wisdom, appointed (you got it) a committee!

The committee pondered that matter and issued its edict, "The new meetinghouse will be built 'on the spot of ground where the old meetinghouse now stands.'"

Amen.

Well, not quite, "Amen."

What happens next is two more town meetings, one in October, one in November. The meetings are to discuss the committee's recommendation.

Everyone hates it. The official vote is to repudiate the committee. Oh, Jeez!

But at the next spring town meeting, a bunch of the most prominent men in town (forty-six of them, in fact) push through a bill to build the new meetinghouse in what is now the lower village.

There was a protest by many of the townspeople, but the powers that be pushed the construction through and before summer was over, they had built the structure under a ledge at the northwest edge of the village.

What happened then was a vote of the town at a meeting in November stating that the town would not pay for the new building nor would they attend services there nor would they pay a minister to preach there.

The boycott lasted one year. The new building was so much better than the old one that peoples' opinions gradually softened and, in August of 1790, they finally voted to accept the inevitable.

And Warner finally had a new meetinghouse . . . by Jeez!

THE PEOPLE

## The Acworth Wild Man

SEEMS THAT IN March of 1925, the Ben Hawkins family was sitting down to a late Sunday dinner in their home over near the Unity town line when one of his daughters looked up to see a scraggly-bearded man looking in their window. The girl screamed and the men folk went for their guns.

The scary man took off with such speed that the men could not catch him. They noted, however, that he was naked except for a pair of shoes and a short raincoat and was over six feet tall.

They reckoned that he was in his early forties with a dark complexion. He was, they said, filthy. Matted wooly hair covered his forehead and eyes.

Now you can imagine what an incident like this did to a town as small as Acworth.

Mrs. I. W. Mailman did her shopping at the general store while carrying a revolver and told everyone that she was ready to use it.

Emily Jeffery was out in her yard one afternoon when the apparition appeared and scared the wits out of her. She called for her three sons who chased him away.

In the chase, they noted that the man easily vaulted over a five-foot fence on their property. He ran, they said, like a deer with his heavy coat flapping at his knees.

No one, it seems, could catch him. Everyone was trying. And all were scared to death. He was the wildest apparition ever seen in Acworth.

Finally, the townsmen formed a posse and scoured the woods for the man. They found his camp over in North Charlestown.

They waited for the man and captured him without incident.

Historian Frank does not tell us what the name of the wild man was but apparently he was harmless and homeless. He had, the historian states, never committed a crime.

He was, no doubt, turned over to the county for care.

# Isaac O. B.

ONE OF THE first attorneys to practice law in the town of Barnstead was one Isaac O. Barnes, Esq.

Lawyer Isaac O. B., as they called him, was a colorful man. He was born in Bedford and educated at Middlebury College and first practiced law in the offices of Titus Brown over in Francestown.

Isaac O. B. was married to Governor Woodbury's sister. He was tall and exceedingly thin and in poor health and moved to the town of Barnstead because of its invigorating air. There his health improved and he, in fact, got very fat.

After nine years he moved on. He went to Lowell where he got into politics. Because of his political clout he got some plum jobs and ended his life as the United States pension agent in Boston.

When in Barnstead, Isaac O. B. lived in a cottage in South Barnstead. As a man of importance, he practiced the law very little but was known and liked for his rapier wit, his fine sense of humor and his biting sarcasm and irony.

There is even a famous poem about Isaac O. Barnes and this is it. It is titled "No Precedent."

> *A jolly fellow was Isaac O. B.*
> *Very large, very fat, very fond of a spree*
> *Very fond of his glass, very fond of a smoke*
> *But fonder by far, than all these, of his joke.*
>
> *To a political barbecue Isaac once went*
> *And with other good fellows the day gaily spent*
> *In eating and drinking . . . which did not agree*
> *With the spacious interior of Isaac O.B.*
>
> *Yet on arriving at home and going to bed*
> *With stomach o'loaded and very light head*
> *He was soon taken ill and was so short of breath*
> *That he thought he was called by the grim angel, death.*
>
> *So he went for a doctor renowned for his skill*
> *Who, hearing that Isaac was fatally ill*
> *Didn't tarry a moment but unto him sped*
> *And found the old gentleman groaning in bed.*

*With feet very hot and his face very red*
*And crying out "Surely I soon shall be dead. . . ."*
*"Oh nonsense . . . pooh, pooh," said the skillful M.D.*
*"Your case is not hopeless, my dear Mr. B."*

*"In fact it's quite simple, the cause is quite plain*
*And you'll soon be as right as a trivet again."*
*"No, doctor," groaned Isaac, "I'm stricken by death,*
*"He's got me now sure . . . oh! I haven't got breath*

*To tell how I suffer." "Oh! Come now Sir, come!"*
*Said the doctor, 'Tis plain you must suffer some*
*But your pulse is not high; you'll come to no harm.*
*For no man ever died with his feet like yours . . . warm!"*

*"I know of a case," gasped Isaac O. B.*
*"So your statement does not at all reassure me.*
*I know of a man and his name I'll repeat*
*John Rogers, the martyr . . . he died with warm feet!"*

# Major Batchelder

THE TOWN OF Nelson back in Colonial times was called Packersfield, and back then it was a much more prominent town than it is today.

The first settler in town was a man named Major Breed Batchelder. He had inherited the land from his father and he and his family had come up from Beverly, Massachusetts, to settle. Major Batchelder was an arrogant man. He let it be known that he and his family were of the gentry and better than the other settlers in town.

When the Revolution began, he continued to support the king and England and even went so far as importing tea from Canada after the boycott and the Boston Tea Party.

Packersfield sent a lot of men to Bunker Hill and many more later to fight under Stark at Bennington. So the *hoi polloi* did not appreciate the good major and, in fact, wanted to try him for treason.

The local Committee of Safety in fact, called him before them and he refused to come. He said he would talk with anyone on his doorstep, but if they set foot in his house, he would infect them with smallpox. I have no idea how he proposed to do this but that is what he is quoted in the history as saying. He then drank to the health of King George. The mob then came after him. But he escaped.

For months, Major Breed Batchelder lived in a cave a quarter of a mile south of his home. His wife used to sneak him food by going a round-about way to the cave and a neighbor, a guy named Jim Phillips, used to leave him a bottle of rum daily in a stream nearby.

Major Batchelder would, of course, sneak back to his home now and again to get a good night's sleep and to see his kids, but, generally, he slept in the cave.

One night the mob came by when they heard he was home. His wife threatened the mob with boiling water and successfully held them off for enough time for her husband to make an escape.

Later, while hiding in his cave, he heard some hunters speculate about what they would do to him if they discovered him. It was so gruesome that Major Batchelder decided to leave town.

His wife told his kids that she was taking them to pick strawberries. When they got to the field, their father appeared to say goodbye.

He was pursued as he left, and he outran the mob up Pinnicle Hill where they were sure he would be cornered. But the major was able to scale down the precipice and get away. To this day that precipice is called Batchelder's Stairs.

He went off to fight with Burgoyne and the British against his own townsmen at the Battle of Bennington. There he caught a musket ball and nearly died.

After the war he went with New Hampshire's last Colonial governor, John Wentworth, to live in Nova Scotia where he became a drunk. He never saw his family again. He died in 1785 by falling out of a boat and drowning.

# The Great Bellows

THIS IS A true story about the great benefactor and founder of the town of Walpole, Colonel Benjamin Bellows.

Colonel Bellows was beloved in the town and was known for his kind heart and generous nature.

After his death, that nature and the affection of the community passed down to his son Thomas, who lived in a place known as the Stagecoach Inn about two miles south of Bellows Falls.

The year of 1816 had probably the worst weather in the history of the country. There was frost in July and crops failed all over America.

People that year actually starved and there was no feed for the livestock, either.

But Thomas Bellows escaped the hardship of that year. His land, being close to the Connecticut River, managed to weather the frosts and cold weather. His farm was one of the few to grow a healthy crop of corn.

Not only that, but Thomas Bellows insisted on selling his corn to those in need at the same price he had charged the year before when there was plenty of corn.

A speculator came by one day and asked the price of Thomas Bellows' corn and was surprised that it was the same as the year before. The man said he would take it all.

"You cannot have it," Thomas Bellows bellowed. "If you need a bushel for your family, you may have it at this price," he said. "But no man can buy from me to speculate in this year of scarcity."

Such was the attitude of a great man who was the son of another great man.

# Ben Chandler Dies on Mt. Washington

ON SUNDAY AFTERNOON, July 18, 1857, a hiker was exploring the summit of Mt. Washington when he came across a human skeleton in the shelter of an overhanging rock. It was about a half mile down from the summit on the north side.

The skeleton was missing its feet and hands. Also part of one arm was gone and the left leg was also missing. Wildcats had gnawed the ribs of the victim. There were some rags and a gold watch. The skull still had long gray hair on it. The gold watch had stopped ticking at ten forty-five. Searchers found the missing leg about thirty feet away from the rest of the bones. They gathered up the remains and packed them on a horse and took them down the mountain to Glen, where the victim's son waited to take his father back to their home in Wilmington, Delaware.

The skeleton was that of 75-year-old Benjamin Chandler.

About a year before, Mr. Chandler had taken the train to the Glen House and late in the afternoon of that same day, he had packed a small bundle of food and clothing and started for the summit of the mountain.

About half way up the mountain, two ministers had passed Mr. Chandler on their way to the Tip Top House. When they arrived, they informed the people there that they had passed an older man and it was unlikely that he would make the summit before darkness fell.

A guide from the house went down the trail, calling out for anyone there. A rainstorm broke and he returned soaked. All agreed that the old man probably turned back and was safe. The next morning, however, a search was made of the summit, just in case. Nothing was heard about the lost man for about a month.

In September, a man named David Chandler arrived in Glen looking for his father. He learned the story and posted a $500 reward for information that might lead to the discovery of his dad. A lot of people went searching that summer but to no avail.

Finally, the next year the skeleton was discovered.

Most think that the old man had been within calling distance of the top when the rainstorm blew in. At that time, he veered off the trail and found an overhanging rock to shelter himself from the storm. He had died that night of exposure, probably about ten forty-five.

# Governor's Calf Pasture

NEW HAMPSHIRE COLONIAL Governor Benning Wentworth was a man who knew how to make deals. Very seldom did anyone get the better of him when it came to business. But the fact is that once in a while he screwed up.

One of these bad decisions involved the deal he made with Colonel Benjamin Bellows during the founding of the town of Walpole. I told this story at the Walpole 250th birthday celebration.

Bellows' first choice of property was where Claremont is. He loved the waterpower there and knew that the land would be great for farming. Unfortunately, it was too far from the "Fort at Number Four" and so had little protection from Native American attacks.

But the land at the falls on the Connecticut River just south of the "Fort at Number Four" had great protection both up and downstream. The land was perfect for farming, and there were times of the year that you could catch salmon with your hands at the waterfall. So he petitioned Governor Benning Wentworth for this land.

Governor Wentworth may have known of Colonel Bellows' reputation because he didn't quite trust him. This is borne out by the Bellows' history.

The story is that there was a certain amount of land in the grant which the governor was to keep for himself, the profits of which would go to the governor's favorite charity. This charity was a missionary society of the Church of England.

The history says:

"It is said that the Governor, in making his selection of land in Walpole, consulted Colonel Bellows as to what was the most favorable portion of the town to lay claim to; expressing his own decided preference to the 500 acres in the immediate neighborhood of the Great Falls as the probable site of the future settlement."

The colonel, very honestly, told him that the land thereabouts would make a very good calf pasture but nothing better.

The governor, perhaps imagining the colonel wished to appropriate these lands for himself, was discouraging his own selection of them, at once resolved to lay his claim there, and his 500 acres on the stony flanks of Stone Mountain were, for some time, called "The Governor's Calf Pasture."

# *Lady Blanche*

BACK DURING THE years between the Civil War and the turn of the century, New Hampshire was home to two of the most important female writers of the time.

No doubt you have heard of Sarah Josepha Hale from Newport. She wrote one of the first American novels, "Northwood," and she went on to become the editor of the largest-selling women's magazine in the country, "Godey's Lady's Book."

The second important New Hampshire female writer came a generation later. She wrote for the *Atlantic Monthly* and for *Galaxy*. In her time, she received more money for her articles than was paid by the same publications to Longfellow or Tennyson or Oliver Wendell Holmes. This woman was a world traveler and highly educated, and she lived the latter part of her life in Conway, New Hampshire.

She was also an English peer, the daughter of Charles, the Second Earl of Gainsborough. In 1848, she had been christened "The Right Honorable Blanch Elizabeth Mary Annunciata Noel."

In this country, she called herself simply, "Blanche," and hers is a story to rival any tragic English novel of her time.

The story begins at the family estate, Exton Hall, in Rutlandshire, England.

Here Lady Blanche grew up amid wealth and position. Her father, the earl, had among his employees an organist for his chapel on the estate. He was a charming Irishman named Thomas Murphy. Murphy was cultured and talented. He spoke languages. He composed. He also was the tutor to the earl's teen-aged daughter. I guess you can figure it out from here.

Love triumphed. But, of course, the earl would not give his permission for such a union and was on the way to fire his organist when . . . you got it . . . the couple eloped. It was 1864, the height of the Civil War, when the sixteen-year-old beauty and her lover sailed for America in the steerage of a sailing ship. They arrived in New York City penniless and bereft. It was here that the Lady commenced her writing career, and her husband got work as a teacher.

Lady Blanche wrote treatises on etiquette and travel. Here's a sample:

> The particular social reserve of Englishmen among themselves has often been the theme of ridicule, and yet, for the same reason which enforces so strict a code of precedence, this precaution seems in a sense far from unnecessary. Of course, it often leads to ludicrous consequences.

And so on.

In 1875, Thomas Murphy and his peeress bride became aware of a teaching position available at the "Kearsarge School for Boys" in North Conway. Here, Thomas Murphy taught music and French, and his wife often substituted for him in class.

The couple managed to save enough money to purchase a lovely cottage with a fine view of the valley. The spot reminded Lady Blanche of her home in the English countryside. And there they lived for more than a dozen years.

But, as with many stories of the time about the sacrifice of money and position for love, this story has a tragic ending.

Although Lady Blanche lived a rigorous outdoor life and walked and gardened, she was not of a robust constitution and, at the age of only thirty-three, she took sick and died. Her beloved husband, Thomas, lived but a few years more and he too passed away.

But their lovely cottage exists to this day on the west side of the Saco River in New Hampshire.

# *John Langdon's Speech*

JOHN LANGDON WAS the first governor of the state of New Hampshire after the Revolution.

The Langdon House in Portsmouth is a state landmark and a state treasure.

The reason I bring his name up is because, in Exeter, is the old meetinghouse in which John Langdon single-handedly, some say, saved the United States.

First of all, John Langdon was among the men who attacked Fort William and Mary in Newcastle in 1774. This raid, and not the Lexington and Concord battle, was the first action of the Revolutionary War. The shot and powder captured from the fort was used in the Battle of Bunker Hill. And that ammunition, legend has it, was secreted under the altar of the Exeter Meetinghouse before it went to Charlestown.

Now back to the story of John Langdon saving the United States.

See, in 1775 and 1776, John Langdon was a member of the Provincial Legislature which met in Exeter . . . Exeter was then the capital of the province. And it was in Exeter that John Langdon learned the news of the fall of Fort Ticonderoga.

We, the Colonists, were losing the war. General Burgoyne had to be stopped, and the only person to do this was General John Stark.

But New Hampshire was broke. There was no money in the public coffers to pay an army. Our credit was completely exhausted.

So there was a meeting in this building and John Langdon felt the gloom and discouragement of his compatriots. And so he went to the pulpit and he said:

"I have a thousand dollars hard money.

"I will pledge my plate for three thousand more.

"I have seventy hogsheads of Tobago Rum which will be sold for the most they will bring. They are at the service of the state.

"If we succeed in defending our firesides and our homes, I may be remunerated.

"If we do not, then the property will be of no value to me.

"Our friend Stark who so nobly maintained the honor of our State at Bunker Hill may safely be entrusted with the honor of the enterprise, and we will check the progress of Burgoyne."

And thus it was that John Langdon almost single-handedly supported General Stark's army which, as we all know, went on to defeat Burgoyne at Bennington and turn the tide of the American Revolution.

And, by the way, John Langdon was the first U.S. senator from New Hampshire, and it was he who had the honor of informing George Washington that he had been elected our first president.

# Lost Lead Mine

ONE OF THE earliest settlers of the town of Bedford was a man named Ephram Bushnell.

Bushnell was a close friend of leader of the community John Goffe, who owned and operated the first mill in the region and for whom the town of Goffstown is named. That being neither here nor there, there is a story about Ephram Bushnell that is told to this day.

Seems in the 1750s, Ephram Bushnell was hunting near his home on the Cohoes Brook near Goffe's Falls when he passed a projecting ledge. Under the ledge, Ephram Bushnell saw a number of stalactite-like drippings.

He took his hatchet from his belt and smote the inverted cones so that they broke off. They were, he discovered, almost pure lead.

As he was stowing the bits of ore in his bag, legend has it, a huge stag appeared. Ephram Bushnell fired his musket and hit the animal but did not bring it down. The deer leaped into the river with Bushnell close on its heels, out the other side, and into the woods with the hunter in pursuit. But Ephram Bushnell was unable to keep up and soon he was lost.

By the end of the day, he found his way home where he told his story and showed his bits of pure lead to Colonel Goffe. The two men melted the lead down and made bullets.

Next day they tried to return to the spot where he had chipped off the pure lead, but he was unable to find it. And for the rest of his life he searched in vain and died never having identified the place.

And to this day people continue to search for the lost Bushnell mine.

So it's near the river and the brook. Maybe you could find it?

# *John Colony*

THE COLONY MILLS MARKETPLACE in Keene is an upscale shopping place with restaurants and lots of ambience. It is called what it is called because this used to be (you got it) the old Colony Mills.

Now Colony is an old and respected name in Keene and over in Harrisville as well.

The original Colony to settle in Keene was John Colony, who came to America from Kilkenny, Ireland, back in 1730. And it was John's grandson, Josiah Colony, who founded the mills there.

John Colony was a member of Robert Rogers Rangers during the French and Indian Wars. He was at the battle of Port Edward when Major Israel Putnam was tied to a tree to be burned. (Major Putnam was not burned that day, but he was terrorized.)

Anyhow, John Colony was strong and brave and smart and energetic. And for his service in the French War, the royal governor gave him a grant of land in Maine. He traded it and made money.

And, finally, he settled in Keene where he wrested a farm out of the wilderness in the western part of town. He married and had four kids and died in 1797.

But, to this day, stories are told about the bravery of John Colony. The Keene town history relates this one:

Seems when John Colony was a young man he was helping to defend a garrison that was surrounded by marauding Indians. In the garrison were a number of women and small children and babies.

The infant children needed milk and John volunteered. He took his musket with his dog and a pail and went out and somehow got through the Indian lines to a cow which he milked.

As he returned to the garrison, the dog barked and John turned to confront a brave with a weapon. Coolly he fired and killed the Indian, but the noise attracted the others and people in the garrison looked out to see John and his dog running like blazes for the garrison with the Indians in hot pursuit.

They opened the door and the young man ran in, and he and others then fired at the pursuers who ran away.

The upshot was that the Indians never got into the garrison. And, incidentally, not a drop of milk was spilt.

And I'll bet that's just what you were wondering. Oh, the dog got away, too.

# The Grandfather Clock

IN THE LATE nineteenth century, John and Mary Dobson left their home in England and boarded a ship bound for Portsmouth, New Hampshire.

Mary had agreed to emigrate as times were bad in jolly old England, and there was promise in America. But she would not leave her home in England without her one great treasure . . . a grandfather clock. It was added expense and bother to crate and send the clock aboard a sailing ship, but John loved his bride and so the clock arrived here with the couple.

In America the couple built a home on a hill overlooking Lake Winnipesaukee. The home was modest . . . just a couple rooms, fireplace, loft . . . and one grand piece of furniture.

The couple soon had a family . . . a baby boy.

One day, John was in the meadows tending the cows when Mary looked out to see four tall Native Americans strolling towards the house.

This was after the Revolutionary War and Indians were no longer a threat, but Mary, like all those in the rural parts of the state, had heard the story of Hannah Dustin and how in a raid the Indians had killed her newborn child simply because it was crying.

Mary was in a panic.

As the Native Americans came up to her door, she picked up her sleeping baby from its cradle and, wrapping it tightly in blankets, she placed the infant in the clock beneath the swinging pendulum.

She then went to the door.

The Indians stood on the doorstep. Mary was so upset she could not speak. One of the braves looked over her shoulder at the pot boiling on the arm over the fire in the fireplace.

As the man looked into the house, the other three pushed past Mary and entered. They began looking into the cupboards and drawers in the dresser. They took nothing but were apparently just curious.

Mary went and stood between the men and the clock. She gestured at the stew on the fire and the bowls on a shelf by the table. The men went and helped themselves.

Mary could hardly breathe. The baby had been quiet but she expected him to awaken any time and begin crying.

The men ate. One strolled over to the clock. It was almost noon. Time for John to come in for lunch.

"Oh God," Mary thought. "The clock is about to chime the noon hour!"

As she thought this, sure enough. The mechanism began whirring to begin the bell. Just as the bell began chiming, Mary let out a scream.

The clock rang. Mary screamed, and from inside the clock the baby began howling.

The Indians leaped back from the clock. It was clearly some evil spirit.

The men quickly ran out of the room just as John came in the back way. He hadn't a clue that anyone had been there.

Everything looked fine. Not much different than when he left earlier in the day . . . except for the four bowls there on the table half-full of soup, and for his wife who was opening up the old clock and taking their baby out of it with tears streaming down her face.

She, of course, told him the story. John, for his part, doubted that the Native Americans would have done any mischief.

But, from that time on, John had a much greater respect for the old clock.

# *Uncle Billy*

BACK BEFORE THERE were phonograph records and tapes and CDs and MP-3s; back before radio and television and films, about the only music people had in their lives they heard in church.

That is, unless the family was wealthy enough to afford a piano.

People didn't hear much music back then.

As a result, often the most popular person in a village was the fiddler.

That was the case in Benton, back in the nineteenth century. From 1843 until his death in 1879, the most popular man in this town was "Uncle" Billy Eastman.

Uncle Billy played the fiddle and sang bass in the choir at the Congregational church. There was never an event in town . . . barn raising or wedding or corn husking that Uncle Billy didn't play his fiddle. He loved to play and to sing, and he loved parties.

Uncle Billy came to Benton in 1843 from Lisbon where he had operated a business that failed.

He also went there because a girl had turned a marriage proposal down from him, and he had a broken heart.

In Benton, Uncle Billy built a mill down on Whitcher brook in Whitcher Hollow near the Amos Whitcher home. (The Whitchers were prominent people in Benton back then.)

The mill Uncle Billy built made spruce clapboards. Everybody needed clapboards for their homes back then.

Uncle Billy's mill prospered and soon he was living in a very fine house, indeed. But living alone, for, alas, when it came to romance, Uncle Billy was very shy and no love came into his life.

Sundays he would sing in church and Saturday nights would play tunes like "The Bumble Bee with His Tail Cut Off" to great applause and laughter.

Uncle Billy trusted everyone and that was his downfall. In the end a lot of people took advantage of him and stole from him and did not pay their bills. The result was that the last years of his life were lived in poverty. His grand house gone . . . his health gone . . . his friends no longer his friends.

He died in his sleep the night of August 6, 1879. He was 85 years old.

## Turned to Stone

CHARLES EMERY WAS in the Army when he died in Washington, D.C. in 1863.

It was during the Civil War. He was twenty-one, a little guy: weighed about 125 pounds.

His body was shipped back to Jaffrey where it was buried in the Conant Cemetery. Then thirteen years later, the body was exhumed and reburied in the Emery family lot.

Now no one knows quite what happened those thirteen years Charles Emery was interred, but when they dug him up they couldn't lift the casket. It finally took eight men to raise the box. It weighed, they said, about 700 pounds.

Inside the body looked normal but it had, they reported, turned to stone. In fact, they reported that his features were recognizable and that his clothing and the flower wreath that was in the casket were perfectly preserved.

Nowadays they would have made tests to see what caused this miraculous thing . . . maybe it was natural salts or minerals in the ground or groundwater that preserved the body and everything else but added hundreds of pounds of weight.

But it being 1876, they just reburied Charlie, and his grave is in the Emery plot.

Another graveyard story in Jaffrey concerns Wilfred Varville's dog, Lassie. This happened about 1970. Alice Varville died, and the dog was left at home during the funeral at St. Patrick's Church.

When the mourners arrived back home after the services, the dog was gone. For two days they searched for the animal to no avail . . . 'til someone visited the cemetery and there, lying amid the flowers on her mistress' grave was Lassie.

Sweet story.

# Joe English Hill

IN NEW BOSTON stands a promontory unique in shape and recognized by all who live in the region, a hill rounded on three sides with a fourth side that falls off in a 300-foot precipice.

This is Joe English Hill.

Joe English, in case you don't know, was a Native American who lived in Colonial times. He was the grandson of Wosconnomet, the Sachem of Agawam.

The Indians themselves gave him his name because he sided with the English when the rest of the Indian nation had declared war on them. After the Councils of Passaconaway and Wonnalancet, Joe English was declared a traitor. Braves all over New England were looking for him, determined he would die.

In 1706, Joe English was hunting alone on a spur of the Uncoonoonuk Range, a place called Ingalls Hill. Suddenly, three Indians appeared. Joe English ran, and the three braves were after him. They chased him to the top of the hill and across through the woods. On the south side of the hill, they almost caught him, but Joe stepped aside and the three fell to their deaths. At least that's the story.

Joe survived a couple years more but, finally, time ran out. Somewhere between Dunstable and Chelmsford, Massachusetts, he and some English friends were ambushed.

Joe ran. He took a bullet in the arm but continued to run. Then a second bullet hit him in the thigh, and he went down. Finally came the coup de grace: a tomahawk embedded in his brain.

But Joe English would not be forgotten. The mountain in New Boston where he escaped death would, from that time on, no longer be called Ingalls Hill. Thenceforth it would be called Joe English Hill, and the Massachusetts Legislature would vote a sum of money and land to be given to his widow and two children because, in the words of the citation: "He died in the service of his country."

Interesting phrase.

# John Fitch

DURING THE FRENCH and Indian Wars, a man named John Fitch built a house and inn out in the wilderness in what is now Ashby, Massachusetts. The house was also used as headquarters for a small garrison of soldiers.

July 5, 1748, was hot. Most of the soldiers were out scouting. Two young soldiers had, however, been left to guard the home.

That day John Fitch, his wife Susannah, and their five children were out in the fields hoeing the crops. By the way, 1748 was during what is called King William's War. In the middle of the afternoon, a dozen or so Indians attacked the garrison. They captured and butchered the two soldiers and burned the house to the ground.

The Indians then went searching for John Fitch and his wife and family. And they found them.

From Massachusetts the party began the trek to Canada where the family would be turned over to the French and ransomed.

Two in the Fitch family were infants. One was just two. He was strapped to the back of an Indian with rawhide laces. The second child was but a few days old. He perished the second day of the march.

In Canada, it was discovered that the two-year-old had lost the use of his legs due to the tight binding that held him to his captor. No circulation got through and although the legs did not have to be amputated, they did not grow and the child never would walk again.

Within a year a ransom was paid, and the Fitch family was put aboard a ship and returned to Providence, Rhode Island. Mrs. Fitch, however, was very ill and died before year's end.

John Fitch himself never recovered from his ordeal. He was poor and depressed to the end of his days.

Now you may wonder why we are telling this story. Well, it's because toward the end of his life John Fitch came to Jaffrey. He moved in with his son Paul, who lived on the hill near the D. D. Bean Company. That part of Jaffrey, by the way, is to this day called Fitch's Corner.

But John Fitch soon became a ward of the town and, in 1789, the constable warned him out of the township.

Broken and alone he returned to Ashby where he died soon afterward.

And that might be the end of the story. But it is not. In fact, there are books and articles and plaques and monuments telling the story of John Fitch and his family. And he also has as lasting a memorial as any person might want, because John Fitch is the man for whom the city of Fitchburg is named.

## Asa Fox, Murderer

THIS IS A story about a young man named Asa Fox who lived in Lebanon in the early 1800s. Asa was mentally disabled.

His father, mother, and sister lived in the family home, but there was another abandoned house on the property. As he grew up, Asa took over a room in this abandoned house and locked it to keep people out. Not that anyone wanted to see what he had in his room.

Asa was violent, and his family, frankly, was scared to death of him. They kept their distance.

About 1830, Asa's father died, and a guardian was appointed to take care of the boy's affairs.

About this time his sister, Hannah, married a local man and moved across town. The new husband, a Mr. Annis, disliked Asa intensely and did not hide his feelings.

About this time Asa came into the possession of an ax. It was not new but it was useful. Asa's brother-in-law took the ax for himself and had a new handle made for it.

Enraged, Asa went and took it back and confronted his brother-in-law and sister as they sat at the breakfast table. The brother-in-law just laughed . . . that is, until Asa took the ax and with two strokes, cut his head off right there at the table.

His sister ran screaming out the door and out into the deep snow. She was headed to the neighbor's house. Asa caught up with her and pointed a pistol at her head and pulled the trigger. The weapon misfired. Asa then took the pistol and clubbed his sister senseless with the butt. He hit her so hard the pistol handle broke off. He then stomped her face into the deep snow and ran home.

Hannah and her husband were buried the next day in the same grave. A posse formed. They went to Asa's house, broke the lock and entered the room. It was filled with stolen goods from friends and family and neighbors: parts of clocks, clothing, parts of guns, paper, kitchen tools.

But Asa wasn't there. They searched the barn and found some glowing coals in a skillet. Apparently, he meant to burn down the barn. But there was no Asa.

A second search, however, turned up a slanted board under the hay in the stable. Under the board was Asa.

He was pretending to be dead.

They carried him to the Lebanon Town Hall and thence to the jail in Haverhill where he continued to pretend to be dead for a number of hours . . . until he became hungry.

The upshot was that because he was, as the court decreed, *non compos mentis* (proof was that he had a guardian), he was kept in jail for the rest of his life, which turned out to be only a half-dozen years.

He and two other inmates managed to escape one winter night. Because it was so cold, Asa came back to the jail. But the exposure had ruined his health, and he died within a few days.

# Daniel Chester French

*This work by its native son stands in Exeter.*

SOLDIER'S MEMORIAL WAS erected in Gale Park in Exeter back in 1922 as a tribute to those who died in World War I.

The work is cast bronze and shows a soldier in France protected by a guardian angel holding the olive branch of peace.

You might pass this memorial a hundred times as I have and fail to notice it.

It was created by a man born in Exeter in 1850. He did not grow up there, however. He grew up in Concord, Massachusetts, where he was friends with, among others, the Alcotts: Bronson, Louisa May and May. May Bronson was a sculptor and she introduced this young man to the form. He turned out to have some talent.

After an apprenticeship with sculptors in Boston and New York, this young man was commissioned by the town of Lexington, Massachusetts, to create a symbol of the American Revolution. It was 1872 and he was just twenty-two. That sculpture is the Minute Man Statue that stands on the Lexington Common.

And the sculptor, who was born in Exeter, was of course, Daniel Chester French.

After creating the Minute Man, Daniel Chester French spent two years in Italy as an apprentice under Thomas Bell. He returned and settled in Stockbridge, Massachusetts, where he lived until his death in 1931.

During that time he returned to Exeter many times.

And he certainly was prolific in his output. At the time of his death he had created more than 250 pieces of sculpture in twenty-one different states, as well as in Paris.

But Daniel Chester French is known mostly for one work that surpasses even the Minute Man statue.

Daniel Chester French is the creator of the most beloved statue in the entire country, the statue of Abraham Lincoln in the Lincoln Memorial in Washington, D.C.

# Leather French

THE MAN'S NICKNAME was "Leather."

He was born in Hollis on September 23, 1781, and christened Stephen Youngman French. For many years he lived as a hermit in a small cabin outside of town.

The Honorary John B. Hill, who wrote the history of Mason, knew French and describes him as a harmless, simple-minded, poverty-stricken person of feeble understanding.

Sometime in his twenties, Stephen French moved to Exeter and took up residence in an area known as "Hurricane," where he built a hut and planted a garden and lived his life out in poverty. Here he dressed solely in tanned sheepskins, which is why townspeople called him "Leather" French. In old age Leather French was resettled in the Exeter Alms House where he died on March 8, 1858 at the age of 77.

And that should be the end of the story, except . . . except for a little volume of poetry by David Barker, a man who knew Leather and created this verse to him:

> *To Leather French*
> *You have haunted the dreams of my sleep Leather French*
> *You have troubled me often and long*
> *And now to give rest to the waves of my soul*
> *Leather French let me sing you a song.*

# Old Soldier Haines

HIS NAME WAS Thomas Haines, and he was known for years around Concord as "Old Soldier Haines." He fought in the American Revolution.

At nineteen, he had been at the retreat from Fort Ticonderoga and had fought in several skirmishes during that retreat and had been slightly wounded.

He kept his Army uniform and proudly displayed the bullet holes in the tunic to anyone who would listen to him.

During one of the battles the British were reinforced by a group of Indians. "Old Soldier Haines" had been pursued by the Indians and had escaped by hiding in a deep ravine.

At the Battle of Bemis Heights, near Saratoga, Thomas Haines was shot in the face. The musket ball traveled through one cheek and exited the other. The wound took out most of his teeth and part of his jaw. He carried the scar to the end of his life. He managed to stay alive after that battle by pretending to be dead. For forty-eight hours he lay amongst the corpses on the battlefield.

For years Old Soldier Haines lived in a small house about four miles outside of Concord on the Chichester Road.

In his old age, he made do with a small pension the government granted him for his service.

He was, according to the history, highly respected in Concord. Despite his grave wound, "Old Soldier Haines" lived until February 13, 1847. He was 87 years old when he died.

## Aaron's Truth and Martha's Shirts

AARON HAND WAS a guy who lived in Benton, back in the mid-nineteenth century.

Aaron was, the town history tells us, shiftless. He preferred fishing, the history says, to work.

Of course, who doesn't? But Aaron Hand seems to have been the laziest man in the county.

He and his family lived out on the old Abraham Norris farm. But he didn't grow anything. He got by with promising work to his neighbors in exchange for food. He'd get the food but never deliver the work.

His wife always said that Aaron would fulfill his obligations as soon as his health improved . . . or when he got the time. She used to say that "Aaron's word was God's truth."

The saying became a local proverb. To this day thereabouts when a person in Benton is suspected of giving someone what we, nowadays, would call "jive," the object of insincerity will say, "Sure, Aaron's word is God's truth."

Another well-remembered character in Benton was Martha Norris. Martha was born in 1806 and died at the age of 82. In her life she made thousands of shirts.

Yes, I said, "Shirts."

See, this was a time when no one had money for store-bought stuff . . . and even if they did have money in a town as small as Benton, there was no place to spend it. Back then people were living close to the wilderness.

Martha was a tailor . . . or sort of a tailor. She sewed by hand and her work held up. She took, the town history says, "honest stitches."

Martha would travel around to different homes in the community and would make shirts for the men and boys of the family out of the homespun cloth, usually wool or linen, that the family made themselves.

Now, as I say, Martha's shirts were strong and long lasting . . . but they were not stylish.

In fact, Martha Norris had only one pattern which she adapted to the size of the customers. The result was that the entire village of Benton wore, as it were, a town uniform.

People from Benton were recognizable at a distance by anyone from any of the adjoining towns. A lot of fun was made of the "Benton Style" which, unfortunately according to the young men, wore like iron.

# Temple Glass

DURING THE AMERICAN Revolution, a man came up from Boston and, way out in the woods of Temple, New Hampshire, he built a factory to make bottles and window glass. It was a great experiment, but it didn't work worth a darn.

The man's name was Robert Hews. He was the son of a prosperous Boston merchant.

During the Revolutionary War, the British blockaded all the American ports. As a result, manufactured goods were in short supply. The reason for that was the Brits had deemed it illegal for Americans to manufacture most items. America, as it were, was to supply the raw materials . . . furs, lumber, wool, cotton . . . but England was to turn this material into goods. And to purchase these goods, Americans were taxed on their import.

Now there were glass factories in the colonies, but they were all illegal and when and if the Brits discovered them they destroyed them.

So now that the war was on, the importation of glass dried up to nothing. It was a perfect time for a start-up. It was a perfect time to cash in on the scarcity.

And Hews was about to cash in. The question of course is, why Temple? The answer is: no one knows. Land was certainly cheap in Temple. Wood for the ovens was plentiful and available. But most manufacturing in those days was located on rivers. Rivers were the cheapest and safest way to get a product to market.

All the roads back then were terrible. And the roads in Temple were especially terrible. Fact is, even today, the road near where the factory was built is bumpy and curvy.

About the only thing going for the site was it was so far out in the woods that the Brits would never find it.

But transporting things as fragile as window glass and bottles in horse-drawn wagons without springs over terrible roads was a guarantee of disaster. These people must have been nuts.

Nevertheless, in 1780 Robert Hews and thirty-two German glassmakers came to Temple and built a glass factory near what is now the Old Nashua Road, about a mile south of the present Route 123.

Right from the beginning it was "Curly, Moe, and Shep start a factory." The first building burned down a month after it was built. It was rebuilt and ten days after production started, again the main furnace cracked because of rain and frost.

Robert Hews persevered, however. He petitioned the state legislature to be exempt from taxes and also to hold a lottery to raise two thousand pounds to rebuild.

The legislature said, "Yes!" but by the time the lottery was held, inflation had eaten up all the profits. Still he managed to rebuild and began turning out bottles. But his workers hated the Temple woods and especially the winters. Soon Robert Hews abandoned the factory and his workers.

The next we hear of Robert Hews is in Boston where he petitioned the Massachusetts Legislature to allow him to hold another lottery to raise money for another glass works, this time in Boston.

And this time it worked. The company became the highly successful Boston Crown Company.

And the thirty-two German glass blowers? They were still in Temple, out of work and on the dole of the town until they were warned out of town by the constable.

And that was the end of the great Temple Glass Factory.

Incidentally, there are shards of glass and broken pieces, but not one complete bottle of Temple Glass has survived.

## Pesky Peter

HIS NAME WAS Peter Howard II. He was born in 1814 and lived in Benton most of his life.

At the age of twenty-five, he married Harriet Tyler and began farming on family land just south of his father's farm and next door to his brother Sam's farm.

But Peter Howard was nothing but trouble. In fact, even as a boy he had been nothing but trouble. His father and his Uncle Daniel had their hands full with him. He lied and stole and connived. His dad, in fact, called him a "pesky rogue."

The name stuck and for the rest of his life people called him Pesky Peter.

His farm was on some of the best land in town and should have been prosperous. But as the town history says, Pesky Peter never "assisted nature" and was never "guilty of work" except when he was forced to do it.

Peter's farm failed. His livestock starved. His crops were not planted. His house roof leaked and was not fixed.

Peter borrowed money from everyone. He traveled miles into other towns to purchase goods on credit from storekeepers who didn't know him. The history says he attended every auction or funeral in the area . . . anywhere there was free food. Like many people then and now, Pesky Peter Howard worked very hard to keep from working.

Peter's wife Harriet bore him three children. She could not cope with life and poverty and died at the age of thirty-seven.

Pesky Peter was glib and pretty good-looking and, like I say, a con man. Soon he had talked another woman into marrying him. His new wife, Emily, came from North Woodstock.

Emily was, the town history tells us, "not brilliant but she had spirit." And she would not put up with Pesky Peter's shenanigans and, now and again, and for the first time in his life, he found himself doing actual work.

He also developed a reputation as a matchmaker. His glibness did wonders in the matchmaking field.

One of his clients, Nathaniel Mulliken, was so pleased with the wife Pesky Peter found for him that he paid Peter an ox yoke . . . and one dollar.

# *Jackwish*

MANY OF US think of tramps and hobos as a relic of the great American Depression of the 1930s. But, truth be known, there were tramps in America way back before there were even railroads.

The Andover town history has a couple stories about tramps coming through that town.

Tramps, by the way, were usually harmless men and women who were averse to regular labor. They would split wood for a meal or would provide entertainment of some sort... singing, dancing, story telling.

Often these kings and queens of the road would travel a regular circuit and, for instance, be in Andover each year the second week in June.

A well-liked tramp called Jim Robinson came through Andover on a regular route for many years. He knew who liked him and would go there for his sustenance.

An old tramp named Sally Keeniston arrived in Andover every spring begging for hard cider which she liked a lot.

One morning in May, Sally was found on the side of the road sleeping it off. From that time on, due to the month and the place she was found, the townspeople of Andover called her "The Mayflower."

An old tramp named "Jackwish" showed up every summer with a bag of tricks and some crude entertainments. He traveled with a cow and a pig. One winter "Jackwish" froze his foot and from that time on, walked on crutches with his foot wrapped in dirty rags.

For five cents, Jackwish could make his cow jump over a stick. For two cents he could make his pig jump over the stick. He noted that the stick was held lower for the pig.

He would pray for five cents and he would give a sermon for fifteen cents. Religion was also entertainment back then.

Jackwish came to Andover for a dozen years. In the end it was painful to see him hobbling down the road accompanied by his two critters.

The last year he came to town was 1844.

It is not known what became of him.

# Lafayette in Bradford

I HAVE DONE stories about the Revolutionary War hero Marquis de Lafayette's tour of the United States back in 1825, one on his visit to Suncook and the other on his visit to Warner.

From Warner, the Marquis was escorted to the Bradford town line while cannons fired a hundred-gun salute. At the line, a contingent from Bradford composed of Captain Allen Cressy, John Harriman, Bartholomew Smith and Dr. Jason H. Ames greeted him. Doctor Ames greeted the old warrior saying, "General Lafayette, we bid thee a hearty welcome to Bradford!"

The company then repaired to the village where old General Abel Blood became so overwrought seeing his old commander that he threw his cocked hat into the Marquis' carriage where it slammed the poor man in the eye and caused some discomfort.

Abel Blood, by the way, had been one of ten men from Bradford who went off to fight in the American Revolution. Blood had been a corporal in Colonel John Stark's company at Bunker Hill.

It was not with some trepidation that General Blood approached the Marquis. He had regaled his fellow townspeople with stories of his wartime service. His friends, especially his closest friend, Andred Aiken, with whom he had served in the war, had told him that Lafayette would probably not remember him.

The hat incident was not an auspicious way to begin, although it did serve to get Lafayette's attention.

The Marquis was then taken into the hall of the Raymond House, a hotel where he sat upon a platform and received greetings from the townsfolk.

Then General Blood approached the Marquis, hat in hand, and Lafayette recognized him at once, not as the man who had hit him in the eye a few minutes before but rather as an old friend and war compatriot.

General Lafayette stepped down from his platform and embraced his old friend, and both men cried openly.

Then General Blood turned to his other old friend and fellow townsperson and crowed, "There, old Aiken, what do you think now?"

Lafayette was a Mason and because of this he was then escorted to the Masonic Lodge where he signed the log. The Masonic Lodge was later housed on the third floor of the Presbury House, another hotel. The Presbury House burned in 1873 and with the fire went the autograph. The Raymond House where Lafayette was received also burned. At the time of the fire in 1897, it was the oldest hotel still in existence in the whole of New England.

The front step from the hotel was later used as a base for the monument erected to Lafayette's visit. And the corners where the event took place are called to this day, "Lafayette Triangle."

# Parson Leavitt

WALPOLE IS AN almost-perfect New England town and is among the prettiest villages in America.

The town also has a grand Colonial history. The founder of the town was Colonel Benjamin Bellows for whom, not incidentally, Bellows Falls, Vermont, is named.

In the eighteenth century, Colonel Bellows was the richest man in the valley... and the most respected. It was he, Colonel Bellows, who hired the first settled minister in Walpole; Parson Leavitt was his name.

Colonel Bellows went first ticket every time he could, and he thought he was hiring a great preacher for the community. But he was so wrong.

Parson Leavitt made a deal with the town and the good colonel that was gold-edged, and that deal would cause a lot of trouble later. The town agreed to pay the minister seventy-five pounds sterling for settlement and a salary of thirty-seven pounds to increase yearly until it reached sixty pounds. That was about double what other towns were offering their ministers.

For this exorbitant sum, the town got an arrogant and vain minister who was, to boot, cruel... and he soon crossed the line in his behavior.

One day, Reverend Leavitt was seen dragging home an African American slave woman whom he owned and who had run away. He had tied a rope to the woman and attached it to his saddle and had pulled her the entire distance dragging on the ground.

The cruelty of the action so offended Colonel Bellows that he vowed the preacher would not stay in his town. Unfortunately, ministers were, in those days, "settled for life" and he held the good colonel up for his entire settlement fee and a year's salary before he would leave.

The town paid it. And the reverend left town.

# Lincoln Speaks

AS YOU NO doubt know, Abraham Lincoln came to New Hampshire in 1860 to visit his son, Robert, who was a student at Philips Exeter Academy.

Lincoln made a stop in New York City on the way up to give a speech at the Cooper Union. This speech was the making of the man, and many feel it was the biggest factor in his nomination for the Republican candidacy for president.

Here in New Hampshire, Lincoln also spoke at a meeting at the Exeter Town Hall and later in Concord and Manchester. In all those places he gave the same talk he had presented in New York.

Many say his voice was not deep and commanding as was Daniel Webster's but that he was, nonetheless a master at the dais.

Of course, the speech itself is one of the most influential in American history. But, more than that, how it was delivered was also important.

One of the Manchester newspapers of the day gave a review of the address that could be used as a text on how to hold an audience. It read:

> His sense of the ludicrous is very keen.
>
> He seems to forget all about himself when talking, and to be entirely engrossed in the welfare of his hearers.
>
> He does not try to show off, to amuse those of his own party, but addresses all his arguments in a way to make new converts.
>
> For the first half hour his opponents would agree with every word he uttered, and from that point he began to lead them off, little by little, cunningly, until it seemed he got them all into his fold.
>
> He displays more shrewdness, more knowledge of the masses of mankind than any public speaker we have heard....

Lincoln was assassinated in 1865.

Edison invented his talking machine in 1877, just a dozen years later. Think of it. If Lincoln had lived we would not have to speculate about his voice or his timing or his accent.

But, hey, they didn't have sound recording but they did have photography and how lucky we all are for that. Just to see that face.

And, who knows? Perhaps the voice might have taken away something from his image.

# Long's Automobile

THE HOLMAN AND Merriman Machine Shop in Hinsdale is an old and venerable business. Been there since Civil War time making bearings and axles and turbines and wheels and factory machine parts of all kinds.

Generations of machinists in this town worked for Holman and Merriman. The company's reputation was solid for miles around.

Now back in Civil War time a guy from Northfield, Massachusetts . . . a guy named George Long, was at a fair over in Brattleboro where he saw a man pedal a kind of grown-up quadracycle . . . that is, a bicycle kind of thing.

Of course steamboats and steam railroads had been around for a couple dozen years by that time, but George got to thinking: Why not make a little steam engine and put it on a kind of four-wheel bicycle frame?

So he experimented. He tried to make a steam engine that ran on kerosene. He tried gunpowder. He tried powdered coal.

What he found was that the hottest fire could be had with charcoal.

By this time, he needed machinery to turn out his idea. And so he came up to the Holman and Merriman Company and rented space and machinery and turned out a very compact and pretty little steam engine.

It all came together in 1879 . . . wood spoke wheels, a solid rear axle and a wheel to steer the contraption.

Top speed? Thirty miles an hour. And it worked! He drove it home to Northfield where the police told him he could not drive on the public way because he scared the horses . . . probably the first traffic citation in U.S. history.

That first automobile is lost to history. Probably disassembled for parts long ago. But Mr. Long was not done yet and he made another vehicle. This time it was a kind of tricycle, with the frame made down in Connecticut at the Albert Pope Bicycle plant.

And this invention of Mr. Long's has gone down in history. It is, in fact, the oldest completely operable self-propelled road vehicle in the Smithsonian Institution.

Go to their web site. There's a picture of it.

And to think it all started in Hinsdale, New Hampshire.

## *Gwin*

HIS NAME WAS Samuel McGowan, and he spoke with a Scottish "burr."

He had this accent because he had lived his first forty years in the north of Scotland in a town called Wicke. There he was a fisherman.

In 1775, the British were having trouble with their American Colonies and privateer ships were stopping English ships and either commandeering them or sinking them.

The British navy needed men.

And so it was that one day a British man-o-war halted Sam's fishing boat and impressed all the men aboard . . . that is to say, shanghaied them into the British navy.

The press gang was put aboard the ship Arabell, bound for Boston. But the Arabell was overtaken by an American privateer, and Samuel McGowan found himself in Boston right at the start of the American Revolution.

There were, of course, no ships out of Boston bound for England or Scotland, and so Sam did the next best thing. He enlisted in the Continental Army and took arms against the government that had stolen him from his home and impressed him in their navy.

After the war, he came north and settled in Cilleyville, in Andover. There he married Dolly, the sister of the founder of the village, Aaron Cilley. They lived in a home just down from the Cilleyville schoolhouse.

In 1818, when Sam was 83 years old, the U.S. government gave him a pension of eight dollars a month.

In town they called him, "Old Gwin," and he was well liked.

He remained in good health well past one hundred years of age, and at the age of 102, the town history tells us, actually ran a horse and plow for several turns over a fairly rough field.

In the end, the town agreed to care for him if he would turn his farm and pension over to them. He agreed. It was a deal that came out very well for him.

Samuel McGowan died in Andover on the first of February 1845. He had lived 110 years, two months, and fifteen days.

There is no stone marking his grave in the Andover Cemetery and that may be because of his beliefs. Asked what religion he was, he would reply, "I am not a Christian but hope to be one... by and by."

# Impaled on a Stake

ON JULY 24TH, 1824, in Bedford, a fifteen-year-old girl, Miss Edie McIntire, was impaled on a stake.

The young woman had been working in a barn on a farm belonging to a man named Thomas Shepard. She was in the hayloft standing on a beam, taking sheaves of rye as they were handed up to her from a farm cart. The cart had stakes on either side to hold the sheaves.

Edie lost her footing and fell eight feet directly onto one of the stakes on the cart. This quote is from the Bedford town history, "The stake first struck on the fleshy part of the ischium and passed laterally into the lower bowels about two inches, thence up through the body in an oblique direction, and out at the left breast."

The town history also tells us that the stake smashed three ribs as it tore through twenty-three inches of the girl's torso and protruded half-a-foot out the top; enough so the poor girl had to hang on it to hold up her weight with her hands while the others broke the stake off at the base. They then carried her into the house, with the stake still embedded, while they awaited Doctor Peter Woodbury.

The stake on which she was impaled was hemlock, freshly cut with the bark skinned off. This made it very slippery . . . which is why it went through the young woman with ease; but the slipperiness also made it much easier to slide the stake out once she was cut down.

Dr. Woodbury noted that when he arrived, he found the girl fully clothed, lying on a bed. Her pulse was barely perceptible. She was panting and in a cold sweat.

They slid the stake out.

Edie's color, the doctor said, was "ghastly." But he noted there was little hemorrhaging and that she seemed not to be in great pain.

He cleaned the entrance and exit wounds and dressed them and (to quote the doctor) "endeavored to excite the system." Frankly, I have no idea what this means. Perhaps whiskey; maybe massage, who knows? The upshot was that her pulse improved and her skin became moist and warmer; in short, she was beginning to come out of shock.

When he left for the night, however, the doctor felt as the family did, that Edie would be dead before morning.

But she did not die. She recovered.

For the next seventeen days she subsisted on a slurry made of cornmeal boiled in water.

Within a couple weeks she was walking. It was noted that her body inclined to the left as she took steps, but she was walking and soon she was walking upright.

Six weeks after the accident she was able to regularly walk sixty rods from her home to attend school.

A year later Dr. Woodbury noted that he saw Edie "robust and happy," living on the farm with the Shepard family.

## *Millerites*

IN THE FIRST half of the nineteenth century, a former Baptist minister from Massachusetts claimed that in studying the Book of Revelation he had worked out the precise date for the second coming of Christ.

Jesus would appear again, he said, between March 21 of 1843 and March 21, 1844.

The man's name was William Miller, and he developed a huge following. Fifty thousand people gave away their earthly wealth. They sewed simple dresses by hand which they called ascension robes and awaited the end of the world and their ascension into heaven.

On the last day of the prophecy all gathered on their rooftops, prayed, sang hymns and rejoiced.

But Christ never came.

Miller went back to the drawing board.

A mistake, he said. A miscalculation. Christ would actually appear on October 22.

Again, the faithful ascended their rooftops in their ascension robes.

And again, the Messiah did not appear.

Now the reason I am telling this story is because one of the biggest groups of Millerites came from New Hampshire . . . specifically from the area around Gilford.

One of the most fervent advocates was Nathaniel Davis, who held camp meetings on Governor's Island in Lake Winnipesaukee. William Miller himself attended one of these meetings in 1840.

Over a half-million people in total came to Millerite camp meetings on the island.

In the winter, the movement also had chapels in Alton and in Lakeview.

Miller's false alarm concerning the second coming was a disappointment to many, if not most of his converts. But many did not give up their belief.

Most of those who stayed with the movement became Seventh Day Adventists, a church which also got its start in the Granite State . . . over in Washington.

# The Hermit of Bow Lake

BACK IN THE 1920S, a hermit lived on Bow Lake in Strafford.

No one seemed to know his name, but they did know he rented a blueberry patch from Nana Waldron and for the entire summer he did not cut his hair or his beard. Townspeople took to calling the hermit "Bluebeard." No one knew where he kept his camp, either.

That is until the spring of 1931, when he bought about three acres of land off Pillsbury Road. There on that lot he constructed a shanty and moved in.

Along with a bed and a makeshift kitchen, the hermit opened an office and a business. He called his business "The Frank Moore's Agency." And so people learned his name, Frank Moore.

The agency was a dating company, help for the lovelorn. Sort of like the dating clubs on the Internet nowadays, but back then, Mr. Moore provided a clearing house for letters. He got people together.

They don't know what he charged for his matchmaking, but he may have succeeded with one couple in Strafford itself. Rumor had it that he arranged the wedding of Widow Hawkes and Charles Streeter.

Every night there used to be a poker game in the back room of Caverly's General Store and one night when the ex-hermit Frank Moore was in the store, the boys invited him into the game. They figured to make some money.

What happened was that the matchmaking hermit was never invited to play again, and the boys were quite a while paying off their IOUs to Mr. Moore.

On January 23, 1947, Frank Moore was walking from his place toward Bow Lake Village when he became dizzy. He climbed off the road and up a snow bank there on Province Road and sat down.

When they found him later he was dead. He was 58 years old... and unmarried.

# *John Morey and the Catamount*

THIS STORY TOOK place back in the mid-nineteenth century in Andover. You'll find it in the town history.

Seems that John Morey and a buddy were out fox hunting up on the shoulder of Kearsarge Mountain one fall day when they suddenly saw their dogs running, not after a fox, but out of the woods directly at them.

Right behind the dogs was a huge mountain lion, a catamount. John's companion joined the dogs hightailing it out of there. John, however aimed his musket at the cat but was afraid of shooting one of his dogs instead.

As the old saying goes, "He who hesitates, is lunch."

And so it was with John Morey.

In an instant, the big cat was upon him, digging his front claws into the man's chest.

Morey grabbed the beast by the throat and squeezed with all his might. At the same time, he took hold of one of the cat's rear legs and held it away from him. The other rear leg, however, was swinging wildly and ripping into his thigh and side. Most of the man's clothing was in shreds, but the cat was weakening as John was a strong man and had not relaxed his grip.

Soon the two, man and beast, were lying on the ground, John bleeding profusely . . . and the cat, dead.

For years Andover parents told the story over and over again to their children, of how John Morey killed the catamount with his bare hands and carried the cat back to town, John all bloody and in rags with the cat's hind legs draped over his shoulders, its head dragging on the ground.

Not much was ever said about his hunting companion, though.

# Murphy's Grave

*Years after his death, the work of Francis Parnell Murphy lives on.*

FRANCIS P. MURPHY is buried in Newport, in St. Patrick's Cemetery, but he has a far bigger monument to himself than the impressive gravestone in the South Cemetery.

Maybe you never heard of him. Many people haven't.

Francis Parnell Murphy was governor of the State of New Hampshire back in the 1930s.

His daddy, Patrick Murphy, was a Civil War hero. Took a bullet in the leg at the Battle of Cedar Creek . . . and went back to march with Sherman to the sea.

After the war, he came back to New England and married and settled in Winchester, New Hampshire. He worked as a tanner and a farmer. Life was very hard. He and his wife Ellen soon had a family. Eight kids. Ellen was a beauty. Both she and Patrick had come from Ireland and were Irish through and through. And, of course, Roman Catholic. And proud. Although the kids didn't have shoes to wear most of the year, they all did very well in the local school. Like their mother, all the kids loved books.

Francis was the middle kid... the fourth of eight and by all accounts the most ambitious. They named him after Saint Francis of Assisi and for Charles Stewart Parnell, the great Irish patriot who fought for home rule.

When Francis was eleven the family packed up and moved to Hudson, Massachusetts, where Patrick got work at the shoe factory there. Within a couple years, Francis, too, was working in the shoe shop. He was making boxes to ship the shoes out on the railroad.

It is hard to explain how difficult it was for a person of Irish descent to be in America in the 1880s. This was a time when the "American Party" was very strong. That was a political party formed simply to limit the immigration of the Irish or any other Roman Catholics. Newspaper "help wanted" ads of the day often featured the initials, NINA which everyone knew meant "No Irish Need Apply."

So this was the America that the teenager Francis Parnell Murphy confronted in the late part of the nineteenth century.

But Francis had his mother's good nature and her ethic for hard work. And he was very bright. And soon he caught the attention of the factory owners who were planning to open a new factory up in Newport, New Hampshire.

To organize the shipping department they sent Francis.

In Newport in June of 1902, Francis Parnell Murphy married Mae Herrick at St. Patrick's Church in a beautiful wedding. Over the years they had five children: Madeleine, Walter, Kathryn, Eleanor and Francis Parnell Jr.

Although the shipping department was run like clockwork, the factory in Newport did not prosper and within three years the owners sold the operation to the W. H. McElwain Company. The only executive the new company kept on was Francis Murphy.

But the new owners didn't do well either and within half-a-dozen years McElwain was ready to shut the operation in Newport down.

Francis Murphy then came to the owners with a proposition: Make him the new superintendent of the operation. What did they have to lose? OK, the bosses said, you got one year.

Within a year Francis Murphy had turned a big money-losing operation into a money-making powerhouse... and he did it like this: First of all, he identified what was wrong. Mostly it was a help problem. Industry was new to Newport and the farmers who worked in the factory would regularly take time off for planting and gathering or whenever else the farm needed them.

What was needed were responsible employees who came to work every day. Francis Murphy knew every employee in the operation. He knew their names and the names of their spouses and children. And he knew their jobs as well as they did.

Here is where the politician-to-be comes to the fore. Murphy talked to all of them individually. Give me full time and on-time work, he said, and if the operation goes well, I'll see you get more money and better conditions. And he kept his word.

The result was a work force that respected him and would go the extra mile when he needed them.

The bosses again took note. He had done so well that they then sent him to Manchester to reorganize their largest plant there. Soon he knew every machine and every last worker there.

The company then built a new plant in Claremont, and Francis Murphy oversaw its construction and was the supervisor of both the Manchester and the Claremont operation.

He was making money and he was getting noted in the greater world. During World War I, he chaired a state public service committee that consolidated and redirected the flow of electricity so that all important war industries in the area had sufficient power to operate at full capacity.

After the war, the McElwain Company merged with The International Shoe Company, and Francis continued to work for them until 1921.

In 1921, his former bosses, the McElwains, came to him with a proposition. They would start a new company and Francis Murphy would be an equal partner.

The upshot was that the poor barefoot boy from Winchester was to become one of the largest shoe manufacturers in the world... and the largest employer in New Hampshire.

By 1940, there were eleven plants in the Granite State and the company employed more than 5,000 workers and turned out more than 100,000,000 pairs of shoes.

What else was there? Well, there was politics. The Murphys now lived in Nashua in a mansion on Concord Street. Francis had served as an aide to Governor Winant and had been a representative in the House . . . chairman of the Ways and Means Committee.

And in 1936 he decided to run for governor himself.

He had a couple strikes against him in the old puritan Granite State. He was Irish. And he was Roman Catholic. No Roman Catholic had ever become governor in the state of New Hampshire.

But Francis Parnell Murphy also had a lot going for him. He was personable. He was extremely smart. He had connections and money. And . . . he was a Republican. Now this last bit of information was not as big an asset in 1936 as it had been in years before.

This was the time of Franklin Delano Roosevelt and the New Deal and, in 1936, even die-hard Republican New Hampshire went for FDR. For Francis Murphy to win, the voters would have to split their tickets.

And split their tickets they did. Francis Parnell Murphy won big time and two years later won a landslide second term.

So . . . a rags to riches story and a New Hampshire story. A few years after Governor Murphy retired, he went into the broadcasting business and he put up the money to create a new radio station in Manchester.

Well, I'll tell you the story about that, but first a little more history.

Now remember . . . after World War II . . . people were impatient for television. Just before the war, TV almost happened, but the war interfered. But in 1948 (just three years after the surrender), WBZ-TV went on the air in Boston, and people rushed to purchase sets.

That was the time when the Federal Communications Commission was giving out band space for proposed stations all over the nation. Problem was that broadcast space was limited to a mere twelve channels in the Very High Frequency band which was what the TVs of the day were equipped to receive. (It would be some years before the UHF frequencies and sets would be around.)

The FCC said that New Hampshire could have just one VHS band, Channel Nine.

And that was it.

But even this one channel was controversial.

Down in Boston the big media people were complaining: "What business did New Hampshire have getting their own channel?"

There were four times as many people living in just the greater Boston area than there were in the entire state of New Hampshire.

In other words, the yokels up here didn't deserve their own TV station. Channel Nine should be assigned to Massachusetts. Some big guns went before the FCC to plead the case: WCOP radio was part of the *Look Magazine* empire ... WHDH was owned by Boston's *Herald Traveler* newspaper ... WLAW was part of the *Lawrence Eagle Tribune* ... Dumont Television ... New England Theaters, Inc. ... were among the dozen entities contesting the FCC decision.

The old Granite State, they said, deserved only UHF channels.

Well, you can imagine what the folks up here in New Hampshire felt.

Of course there were half-a-dozen entities in the Granite State as well that also were vying for the open channel.

WKBK Radio, being the most successful radio station in the state, thought that they had the inside track. They had property on Uncanoonuc Mountain for the transmitter. In their confidence, they even built a television studio into their new radio-station building on Front Street.

New Hampshire's oldest operating station, WFEA, also had applied for a license for the channel.

So did radio station WMUR which, not incidentally, was owned by our old friend Governor Francis Parnell Murphy.

Even the *Union Leader* newspaper was in the running for the station.

But when the attack came from Massachusetts, differences were put on the back burner and pressure was exerted in Washington through the state's congressmen and senators.

Senator Styles Bridges was as powerful a senator as the country had and Senator Charles Toby had represented New Hampshire for years. Also Reps. Chester Merrow and Norris Cotton had clout in Washington, D.C.

The upshot was that the license for the new channel was awarded to "Radio Voice of New Hampshire, Inc." which was . . . Francis P. Murphy's company.

No one knows if the governor had any special pressure brought to bear in order to receive the license. Or if it was the fact that, like KBK, Murphy's radio station already had a broadcasting tower on Uncanoonuc. It was, in fact, an FM tower.

And so, at four o'clock in the afternoon on March 26, 1954, WMUR TV signed on the air from their radio-station studios on Upper Elm Street in Manchester.

The living room of the old Victorian house served as studios. Two cameras. And the on-air talent came mostly from the radio station or from other radio stations in the city.

And that was the start of it all.

I said at the start of this story that Francis Parnell Murphy had an even bigger monument to himself than the impressive gravestone in St. Patrick's Cemetery in Newport . . . and that monument is, of course, . . . not the tower itself (although it is impressive) but the station that for more than fifty years has served the people of the Old Granite State and millions of others as well.

Governor Murphy died four years after the station went on the air. By then the radio station had been sold and its call letters changed from WMUR to WGIR.

And that's about the story.

Except there is, in one of the engineering studios at Channel Nine, a large black-and-white photograph on the wall in a corner of the room. Until lately most people in the station even, did not know that this was Francis Murphy . . . nor did they know that the call letters of the TV station are the first three letters of his name.

This is Murphy TV: M.U.R.

# Nancy

HER NAME WAS simply, "Nancy." She was a slave in Concord, New Hampshire.

It is hard to realize that there was slavery in New Hampshire once upon a time, but there was.

A man from Bow purchased Nancy in Boston back in 1766 and brought her home.

When the child was two years old, the man sold her to Lieutenant Richard Herbert in Concord. He got five dollars for the baby and presumably made a profit.

Lieutenant Herbert was a shoemaker and, later on, had a malt business. He was to fight with General John Stark at the Battle of Bennington, which is where he got his military title.

He had a large family in Concord and treated the slave, Nancy, like one of his daughters. She ate with the family and was sent to school and learned to read and write and say her catechisms. From her own recount, she was never made to feel inferior or to wish that she had been born white.

However, when the New Hampshire State Constitution was adopted in 1783, it abolished slavery within the state.

Nancy was fifteen at the time. She had been told that she had come from Boston and somehow she thought that, should she be freed, she would have to return there. She had asked people in Concord which road led to Boston.

One day she was washing dishes when a neighbor burst in to tell her that the Constitution was signed and she was free!

Nancy burst into tears. "What shall become of me?" she said.

The family gathered around and assured her she would not have to leave them. They told her of their love for her and that she would still have her old room. They immediately came to an agreement on a sum she should be paid for her labors.

Nancy stayed with the Herbert family and never married. After Mrs. Herbert's death and through a provision in her will, she stayed with the family of one of the sons through her whole life.

# The Witch of Salem

NOW MOST EVERYONE has heard of the Salem witches. In fact, the witch Rebecca Nurse is a blood ancestor of mine. So I am always interested in witches... especially Salem witches.

Well, it turns out not only was there purported witchcraft in Salem, Massachusetts, there was also a purported witch in Salem, New Hampshire. Her name was Grannie Ober and, back during the time of the American Revolution, she lived with her grandson John Ober in what is now Salem.

Granny Ober used to walk a mile or so to her neighbors, the Wheelers, to purchase milk. One day Granny Ober arrived and was told by Mrs. Wheeler, Esther, that she could not spare any milk that day. Grannie was livid. She had walked all that distance. The least they could do was spare a cup or two. In her anger Granny stormed from the Wheeler house shouting, "You'll be sorry!"

And so they were. The next morning Esther Wheeler went out to milk her cow only to find the animal flat on her back with her feet in the air as if dead. She called the neighbors and they got the old cow up, for she was not dead. The next morning the cow was all right but the third day she was flat on her back again.

Clearly, Granny Ober had bewitched the animal.

Esther Wheeler rushed into her house and emerged with a carving knife. She then took a piece of the cow's tail and ears and brought them into the kitchen. There, at the fire, she threw the ears and tail into the coals and held them down with a poker. "They sputtered and blazed terribly," Mrs. Wheeler is quoted in the town history as saying.

The next day Esther's brother, Abner, who lived next door, came by and said, "Did you hear the news? Granny Ober fell into a bush and scratched herself terrible and then it caught fire and she burned to death... burned her ears off, it did."

The Salem town history notes that, "Doubtless the cow was not further troubled."

And that is the story of the Salem witch from New Hampshire.

# Lyndeborough Silver Mine

BETTER THAN TWO hundred years ago, in the spring of 1783, a man came up to Lyneborough from Medway, Massachusetts, and convinced the natives that there was silver under their land.

The man was Joshua Partridge, and he was a dowser. Yes, just like the dowsers who find water with a divining rod, so Joshua Partridge could, he said, detect precious metals. And Mr. Partridge set about dowsing the area. The result was the Great Scataquog Hill Silver Mine.

Scataquog Hill is the last of a string of hills in Lyndeborough, the others being Winn Mountain, Rose Mountain, Lyndeborough Mountain and the Pinnacle. The next peak is Piscataquog Hill, called back then simply, Scataquog.

Mr. Partridge found, he said, a vein of silver ore near the top of the mountain on land belonging to Francis Epes. Twenty-four shares of stock in the operation were sold to some twenty townsmen. Sixty-four pounds in all, a great sum back then.

Between April and June, the company blasted a deep ditch and tunnel into the summit of the hill. Lots of volunteer help came in the hopes of sharing in the find.

But, alas, there was no silver. The biggest loser was Francis Epes, the property owner. He lost thirteen pounds. The rest of the investors lost only a pound or two apiece.

Colonel Hutchinson, the Lyndeborough town history tells us, had provided rum, blasting powder, sugar and coffee to the workers and he was out, he figured, two pounds-fourteen.

And that was the end of the only silver mine ever to be dug in Lyndeborough.

I say, no one found any silver. Actually, Joshua Partridge, the dowser, left town with a great deal of silver.

## Commodore Perkins

*The memorial to Commodore Perkins can be found on the west side of the State House in Concord.*

GEORGE HAMILTON PERKINS was born over in Hopkinton in December of 1835.

His granddad, Roger Perkins, was one of the first setters of the town and his great-uncle, Brimsley Perkins, ran a popular tavern in the town. George's dad was a judge. And Judge Perkins was the person who founded the village of Contoocook, which you may know, is still a part of Hopkinton.

So George Hamilton Perkins' lineage, in New Hampshire terms, was important.

In the early 1850s George went off to the U.S. Naval Academy at Annapolis.

At the start of the Civil War, he was commissioned a first lieutenant and named executive officer on the *USS Cayuga*.

A year later the *Cayuga* was part of the capture of New Orleans.

Lieutenant Perkins went ashore with Captain Theodorus Bailey to accept the surrender of the city. As the men marched through the streets, the citizens of the city threw garbage on them from rooftops, pelted them with stones and threatened them with knives and pistols.

No one was killed, however.

After New Orleans, Perkins was promoted to lieutenant commander and given command of the gunboat *New London*. For months his boat ran powder and dispatches between New Orleans and Baton Rouge. During this time, there were many skirmishes between the New London and Confederate ships that cruised the waters off Louisiana.

During the next year, Perkins served on the *Scioto*, hunting blockade runners. He was relieved in 1864 and told he could return north to his family.

Instead he immediately volunteered at the battle of Mobile Bay. He was given command of the *USS Chickasaw*.

During this fierce battle at Mobile Bay, one of the Union ironclads was sunk by the Confederates. All aboard the ship were lost, but the day was won by the Union side and Commander Perkins was cited for his valor, especially in the disabling of the Confederate ship, *Tennessee*.

In fact, Admiral Farragut himself, in his official report of the battle, said, "I cannot give too much praise to Lieutenant Commander Perkins who, although he had orders to return North, volunteered to take command of the *Chickasaw* and did his duty nobly." He also said that he was the bravest man that ever trod the deck of a ship.

By the end of the war, Perkins was a full commander. In 1882, he was commissioned captain and in 1896 was made a commodore.

He remains one of the heroes of the Civil War and the greatest naval hero of that war to come from the Granite State.

In 1902, a statue of Commodore Perkins was unveiled on the west side of the New Hampshire State Capitol. The statue was carved by Daniel Chester French, who also came from New Hampshire . . . Exeter.

French also created the Minute Man Memorial on the green in Lexington and the great statue of Abraham Lincoln in the Lincoln Memorial in Washington, D.C.

## *Over to Satan*

BACK IN THE late eighteenth century, the town of Croydon got a new minister, a Reverend Ballard.

Reverend Ballard was a hellfire-and-brimstone preacher and proved popular with much of his congregation. One of those who took the new preacher seriously was one of the first settlers of the town, Ezekiel Powers.

Reverend Ballard ran his church with a steely hand. People were on time, and they prayed and obeyed the rules. One of those rules was that of keeping the Sabbath. No work was to be done and, of course, no pleasures were to be taken up. That included social visiting. And the rules applied to entire families in the church.

Well, "Zeke" Powers called a meeting of his family and told them that they would henceforth obey all the rules of the church or suffer the consequences. This was all well and good except for Zeke's oldest son, also named Zeke.

Zeke Jr. was sixteen and was afflicted with raging hormones. And on a Sunday night, young Zeke went a sparkin' with a neighbor's daughter and didn't get home until breakfast Monday.

Zeke Sr. grabbed Zeke Jr. by the collar and shook him severely. He then took a buggy whip to him and told him if he ever went a sparkin' on a Sunday again he would whip his hide right off.

Zeke Sr. was a big man, over six feet. But Zeke Jr. was even bigger, and he defied his father. Told him that he would go a sparkin' any time he had a mind to.

Well, that was it.

Next Sunday after the Reverend Ballard had completed his sermon, Zeke Sr. stood up.

With tears streaming down his cheeks he addressed the congregation.

"Brothers and Sisters," he said, "I arise to perform a painful duty to my family, to the church, and to my God. My son Ezekiel has proved incorrigible. Sunday night he went a courtin'. It distresses me to say it, but I consent to heave him over to the buffetings of Satan!"

And that was almost that. Zeke had consigned his own son to hell.

I say, "almost" because, at that moment in church, Ezra Cooper also stood up and cried out, "Heave my son Jonathan over with him . . . he went a sparkin' Sunday night, too!"

Such were the tribulations in Croydon, New Hampshire, in the late seventeen hundreds.

# The First Man to Die at Number Four

*Fort Number Four is in Charlestown.*

THE FIRST MAN to die at Fort Number Four during the French and Indian Wars was Seth Putnam. It was the second of May 1746. It was evening.

Seth and a few soldiers from the fort were accompanying some of the women as they went out to milk the cows. A few hundred yards from the fort, a group of eight Native Americans suddenly stood up from behind a log and fired muskets.

Seth fell dead. The Indians fell forward to scalp him, but Major Josiah Willard and his men fired and killed two of the braves and the rest fled.

As it was the first salvo of the war, the killing of Seth Putnam was talked about all over New England. At the fort it was the only subject of conversation and people were on edge.

Three weeks later the fort was fortified by the arrival of Captain Daniel Paine and a troop of mounted soldiers. Captain Paine wanted to see the place where Seth Putnam was killed.

Captain Phineas Stevens was the commander of the soldiers who had been there at the fort before the arrival of the cavalry. Captain Stevens was an experienced Indian fighter and he told Captain Paine that to go back to the site of the killing could be a mistake. It was just the thing that the Native Americans would expect the settlers to do.

"Nonsense," Captain Paine said, "or, at least highly improbable. Who is coming with me?"

It ended up that many of the new arrivals wanted to go and also many of the people who had been living there near the fort as well.

And off they went.

There at the site of the killing the Indians were waiting and, while the group was contemplating the place, the trap was sprung.

The Native Americans had let the party pass so that when they jumped up the party would have to go through them to get back to the fort.

The ambush began. Elijah Allen, Peter Perin, Aaron Lyon and Joseph Massey were shot dead where they stood. Ensign Obadiah Sartwell was run down and taken prisoner. Sam Farnesworth was pursued also by the braves and almost got away when one of the pursuers got hold of his shirt.

The Indian grabbed Sam's throat when a shot rang out. One of the soldiers attempted to kill the Indian but his mark was off, and the musket ball hit Sam in the head and killed him.

About this time, Captain Stevens arrived with a group of soldiers from the fort that began picking off the attackers. The Native Americans gave up the battle, running off and leaving blankets and a number of firearms.

The soldier who killed Sam Farnesworth was not charged, and Ensign Sartwell was taken to Canada where he was ransomed by the French. He returned to the fort in August of the next year.

And this was the start of the French and Indian War in the Connecticut River Valley.

# Priscilla Quimby's Ghost

MOSES QUIMBY WAS a good man. Revolutionary War veteran. Father of two small children and a well-liked member of the Lancaster community.

One day he marched with the local militia down to a military muster in Lisbon. Moses was loading the cannon on the training field and the thing exploded. Moses' wife, Priscilla, was now a widow.

Back in those days there was little if any employment for a woman, and Priscilla did what she could to eke out enough to feed her family . . . sewing and selling eggs and the like, mostly.

Now it turns out there was a haunted house in Lancaster. It was owned by a man named Simeon Spooner. The house was falling to wrack and ruin because he could not rent it. Every time someone moved in, there would be a terrible screeching, like a banshee from the grave and the tenants would move out.

Simeon knew of the widow's plight, and he made her an offer. She and the two kids could live in the haunted house, if they could stand it, rent free. The only provision was that she stay there and make what improvements she could to the property.

Priscilla moved right in. Sure enough a week went by, and then one night there was a terrible wailing coming from the upstairs of the house.

The children were asleep and Priscilla was alone . . . and scared to death. But she knew she could not leave the house. She had no choice. And so, instead of hiding from the horrible noise, she lit a candle and walked up the stairs toward it. The howling was coming from an empty rear room. She blew out the candle because she felt that if it were a supernatural thing, she could discover it better in the dark.

She entered the room. The howling stopped. And then it began again, softly at first. She could not determine where it was coming from. As it grew louder, she walked toward it. It was outside the window. The shadows showed that something was trying to get in the second-story window.

Priscilla sprang to the middle of the casing. Whatever it was, was not getting away.

What she saw was this.

A branch of an ancient tree was scraping and scratching over the roof and windowpanes as it blew back and forth in the wind.

The next day Priscilla asked a neighbor to cut the limb off the tree. He did so.

And the ghost disappeared.

## The Sea Captain

JOHN ROACH WAS an Irishman. Came from Cork and went to sea as a lad. In 1778, he was forty-one. By this time he had advanced to being a captain of a merchant ship sailing out of Quebec taking furs to London.

Captain Roach was, the Concord town history tells us, a shady character. The many anecdotes about him, the history says, "Illustrate his vices rather than his virtues."

His arrival here in the Colonies may illustrate that. See, Captain Roach told people he got off course (that is, lost), sailing from Canada to England and he ended up, not in London but in Portsmouth where, so it wasn't a total loss, he sold his cargo of furs locally and pocketed the profit. Sold the ship, too.

With his new wealth, he then married Major Robert Rogers' ex-wife. Her maiden name had been Elizabeth Furness and she had—and this is pretty scandalous too—she had divorced the major. The charges in the divorce are not known, but what is known is that Elizabeth was good-looking and had money of her own. In other words, a catch for someone with as liberal an outlook as Captain Roach.

The wags were talking in Portsmouth and so the couple moved to Concord where they purchased a large home and farm. The farm was later the home of Governor Isaac Hill.

Elizabeth and Captain Roach were wealthy, but they were not socially connected. The Captain spent most of his time in Concord in Mother Osgood's Tavern drinking flip. The locals would play jokes on the man by making small holes in his rum kegs so the liquor would leak out.

They did this, the history tells us, in order to hear him swear. Apparently, he was very good at strong oaths.

Captain Roach died in his sleep at home on May 11, 1811. He was 74.

In his eulogy, they mentioned his virtues rather than his vices.

It was a very short service.

# Doctor Robb

ON SEPTEMBER 1, 1923, a local man noticed a trunk floating in the Merrimack River by the Tyngsboro, Massachusetts, bridge.

He pulled it out of the water and opened it.

Inside was the torso of a woman. There were no arms or legs or head.

The next day another trunk was pulled from the river. Inside that trunk were the arms and legs of the same woman. But there was still no head.

The newspapers had a field day. They dubbed it the "Suitcase Murder."

People with missing daughters and wives from all over New England came forward to see if the body belonged to their family. One man claimed it was his runaway wife . . . until she was found waiting tables in a Keene restaurant.

But the family of Alice Wolschendorf had a different story. Alice's husband made a positive identification. His wife had been missing ever since she had checked in to Dr. William Robb's clinic in Boston.

Dr. Robb performed abortions.

Now the reason we are telling this story is that back around 1912, Dr. William Robb and his brother Frank had operated a sanitarium in Marlow. Also, Dr. Robb was married to a local woman, the daughter of Mrs. George Petts, who lived there. Later Dr. Robb and his brother moved to Keene and operated their practice.

Brother Frank, by the way, was a trained nurse.

In 1917, the Cheshire Medical Society revoked Dr. Robb's license to practice medicine in New Hampshire. He was charged with malpractice . . . performing abortions.

Dr. Robb and brother Frank then moved to Boston where they opened another clinic.

Then the trunks were pulled from the river.

Seems that the dead woman, Mrs. Wolschendorf, had been a driver for a securities salesman, a William Bowen. The police visited Mr. Bowen and got the story.

Bowen was a bachelor and a good-looking man. Mrs. Wolschendorf found herself pregnant and didn't deem it right to tell her husband. Bowen knew of Dr. Robb's sanitarium.

And Mrs Wolschendorf checked in ... and checked out, as it were.

Mr. Bowen, too, tried to check out ... he attempted suicide, but failed.

So Dr. Robb was wanted by the police, but he was nowhere to be found. His wife told police he had gone to New York for a vacation.

Later he turned himself in to police in Cambridge, Massachusetts.

On the 19th of September, the grand jury indicted Dr. Robb for murder. His lawyers challenged the charge and got it reduced to a charge of performing an illegal abortion.

On December 7, Dr. William Robb pleaded guilty to the charge. He was sentenced to five to seven years in prison. He also conducted police to the place where they dug up the woman's head.

The story was very simple, a botched abortion. Mrs. Wolschendorf had died on the operating table, and Dr. Robb and an associate had cut her up and carried her to the river in a couple of trunks.

When Dr. Robb was released from prison, he came back to Marlow where he was given permission from the Cheshire Medical Board to operate a limited family practice.

And to the end of his days, William Robb was remembered fondly as this town's kindly old country doctor.

# Romeo and Juliet

THIS STORY IS reputed to be true and is in the Andover town history. It is a bit frustrating in that the names of the people in the tale are not revealed. But it is a great story.

The time was 1810. Over in New York State, a young couple got married. He was twenty years old and she only sixteen. Very young, although, in those days, not uncommon.

Soon she was pregnant. But he could not support the family. One day he was gone. Off to join the Army. His intention was to send part of his paycheck home.

But her family would have none of it. They were so angry that they would not allow their daughter to even correspond with her husband.

The young mother moved in with friends and comfortably lived for a number of years.

A year of so after starting her new life she received news that her husband had died in the Army. And so she re-married and lived in New York until 1852, when she became a widow again. Her daughter had, by then, married a Doctor Durkee and moved to Andover.

A year later, the mother boarded a train to come and stay with her daughter. On the way, she happened to sit beside an elderly gentleman who also was on the way to Andover.

At the station, the two older people stopped a passerby. "Could you tell me," she asked, "the way to the home of Doctor Durkee, for his wife is my daughter."

The old gentleman paled. "But," he said, "Doctor Durkee's wife is my daughter as well."

True story, they say.

And, according to the town history, on Thanksgiving Day, 1853, the Reverend Oliver Butler stood at the altar at the Congregational Church and remarried the couple.

The history notes that it is supposed that they lived "happily" if not long, "ever after."

# Ed Shedd

EVERY TOWN IN New Hampshire has stories about local characters.

Such a character was Ed Shedd.

Ed was a guy who lived in Stoddard during the second half of the nineteenth century and the first third of the twentieth.

Ed Shedd was one cheap son of a gun. Even in a parsimonious town like Stoddard, Ed stood out and stories about his frugality are legion.

Ed didn't ride a bus or railroad, never hired a horse. He walked everywhere. Once he walked all the way to Lowell, Massachusetts, by way of Milford, New Hampshire, and the entire trip cost him a total of fifteen cents which he spent on crackers. That was all he ate on the entire trip of a couple hundred miles.

This is not to say Ed Shedd never rode a railroad. He did. In his youth he would hobo it . . . that is, hop freights to visit various places out west.

Ed kept his money in sixteen different banks. Once he set out to walk to Keene to deposit $1,500 in a bank there.

The story goes that word of his trip got to some highwaymen and they waited for him near Keene on the top of Concord Hill. They waited and waited. All that passed was an old tramp.

Sure enough, a prosperous well-dressed guy came up the road and the robbers pounced on him.

The man had a total of fifteen cents.

Well, you guessed it; the tramp was Ed and by the time the crooks figured it out, the $1,500 was in the bank.

Of course, Ed never spent money on clothes. He dressed in old pants and went barefoot in all but the coldest weather. Then he wore just an old pair of rubbers. Even in the wintertime he spurned overcoats.

In his old age, Ed Shedd lived alone. In 1930, people noted that they had not seen Ed for some time and some friends went out to his house to see what was up. What was up wasn't Ed Shedd. Ed Shedd, in fact, was down. He had suffered a fall and had broken his leg and was still lying on the floor of his kitchen.

His friends took him to the Elliot Hospital in Keene. There he got a lot of attention from the nurses and staff. Ed Shedd liked the attention and lived the next four years there in the hospital.

He died in February of 1934 at the age of eighty-five. He left his estate to the hospital . . . better than $54,000, a lot of money in 1934.

To this day the W. E. Shedd Fund provides income to the Keene hospital.

## AWOL: John Starburd

JOHN STARBURD WAS filled with patriotic fervor. The War of 1812 got his dander up, and he decided to join the Army. That meant a walk to Portsmouth where the recruiting office was, and so the young man set off to do his duty.

Problem was, John Starburd had not been away from home for any length of time before, and like millions before him and millions after him, John Starburd got homesick. The upshot was that his neighbors in Strafford began seeing him . . . on the road and in the general store. Soldier Starburd was absent without leave from the Army.

But the times being what they were and Yankees being what they are, no one mentioned to John that anything was wrong. That is, until the representatives of the Army in Portsmouth came to town and ordered John's neighbors, Pomfret Perry and John Sewards, to be deputized and to bring the dissenter in!

Easier ordered, it turns out, than done.

That night the two neighbors found John on the road and had a talk with him. "Go back," they said. "It'll be a lot easier."

"Mind your own business!" John said. And that was that.

Next morning Perry and Sewards arrived at Starburd's front door fully expecting to have to use force to do their duty.

Starburd flung open the door, greeted his visitors, and pushed them aside and ran down the road and over the fields.

He ran through the briers and he ran through the swamp, he ran over stone walls and brooks.

Whenever it appeared the pursuers were about to catch up, Starburd would put on a new burst of speed and outrun them.

He was good!

Soon the pursuers were gasping for air and hopelessly outrun.

Next day they came back. Same thing happened. And the next day. And the next. They tried the evening and the same thing happened, Starburd got away and outran them.

This went on for a week or so and then . . . and then an odd thing happened.

One day the pursuers came to his house, and he was not there. John Starburd had returned to Portsmouth and the Army.

Later they learned that the word of Starburd's exploits had not gone unrecognized by the Army... and the only punishment he received was a little extra guard duty.

## Molly Stark's Cannon

*"Old Molly" can still be found today in New Hampshire.*

AT DAWN ON August 16, 1777, New Hampshire General John Stark prepared to assault a detachment of General Burgoyne's British troops at Bennington, Vermont.

General Stark was a fine fighter and held his positions at Bunker Hill. But he was rough and plainspoken and the aristocracy of the day sneered at his crudeness. Due to his breeding, he was passed over for promotion, although his men knew he was the finest fighter on the American side.

He was at Bennington because the Colonists came to realize he was the only man who could inspire great loyalty among the troops.

Stark had agreed to lead the troops with the provision that he be paid by the State of New Hampshire and that he answer to no one but himself. The legislature in Exeter had agreed to his demands.

The morning of the battle, Stark saw the temporary fort on the hill overlooking the Wallomsac River and he called out to his troops, "There are the Redcoats and Torries! They are ours or Molly Stark sleeps a widow tonight!"

The victory was quick and bloody. The British commander was killed and only a few of his troops escaped.

Thus was won the first battle of Walloomsac. Many historians count this battle as the major turning point in the American Revolution. First of all, it was a victory at a time when a victory was sorely needed. And secondly, the battle was won by a militia. Up to that time, even the Colonials regarded the militia as second-rate when up against His Majesty's highly trained army. And it was true that, before this battle, militias had been poorly trained, unruly and nearly impossible to command. The American troops at Bennington fought better than the British troops that day. And they were held together that day by the great respect in which they held their leader, General Stark.

Along with prisoners and position, the militia also captured guns and ammunition, including the French cannon, state-of-the-art for its time. This cannon is now in the New Boston Historical Society rooms.

The cannon is cast of solid brass and it has a history that predates and postdates the Battle of Bennington.

Originally the gun belonged to the French army, the army of General Montcalm. But the English general, James Wolfe, captured the gun during the battle on the Plains of Abraham outside Quebec in the French and Indian War. That battle is commemorated, as you probably know, in the great painting titled *The Death of Wolfe*, by the artist Benjamin West. General Wolfe was lost, but the cannon was one of a pair that was captured, only to be lost again at Bennington.

So the Americans now had the guns. The English, however, were to get them back. The recapture occurred in Detroit during the War of 1812. But then the Americans took the guns back; in the same war at the Battle of Fort George.

The other gun, the mate of this one, was fitted out on an American privateer, a pirate ship, during the War of 1812. The ship was sunk and the gun went with it.

But this gun survives. Think of it. It served once under the French, twice under the English and twice under the Americans.

So why is it in New Boston? Well, we don't know. But many of the men who followed Stark to Bennington came from that town, and it is assumed that the general himself gave the gun to the local militia, the New Boston Artillery Company. And there it has stayed.

And for two hundred years now this cannon has been called after General Stark's great inspiration; the inspiration which many say won the battle of Bennington that day. The cannon is called Old Molly.

## *The Other John Stark*

NO DOUBT YOU know about New Hampshire's greatest Revolutionary War hero, John Stark.

But do you know about the John Stark who fought for the British during the Revolutionary War?

General Stark was the hero of Bunker Hill and of the Battle of Bennington and is the originator of the slogan on New Hampshire's license plates, "Live Free or Die." Without Stark's victory at Bennington, many historians feel we might not have won the war.

But John Stark had a brother, William. And William was a proud man. He was a colonel in the state militia, and he had fought bravely in the French and Indian Wars.

Colonel William Stark volunteered to raise and command a regiment to fight against the British. But the New Hampshire General Assembly in Exeter was filled with snobs, and William Stark was a fine soldier but he was crude in language and manners. Instead, the Assembly voted to give the assignment to Colonel Hobart who Stark knew to be a fool and pretender.

William's son, John, had been named for his uncle, and he was angered by the snub given his father and he became a radical Tory. Playing on his father's anger, he persuaded his dad to also come over to the Tory cause.

William did just this and soon there was an arrest warrant issued commanding him to come to court to face charges of counterfeiting there in his home town of Dunbarton.

Seems the charges had merit and William and John skipped town. They left William's wife and five children to fend for themselves.

The father and son ended up on Long Island where William successfully recruited a contingent of 250 Colonists to fight for the British cause. He was appointed a lieutenant colonel in the British army.

He died six years later of a heart attack while watching a polo game.

His wife Mary, back in Dunbarton, it is said, went mad when she heard the news. With five children to feed and no income, life had been hard and the community had been no help at all. The family was branded as traitors and people went out of their way to make things disagreeable for them in the hopes that they would move. But there was no place to go.

After the war, John emigrated to Nova Scotia and then to what is now New Brunswick. Years later he returned for a visit to Dunbarton, where he found his mother and sister living in dire squalor. The neighbors did not appreciate John's return, and he soon gave his mother what money he had and left town.

# *John Taggert's Journey*

JOHN TAGGERT WAS born in Londonderry, Ireland, in 1721. As a young man he was part of the Scots-Irish emigration to Derry, New Hampshire.

From Derry, John Taggert moved first to Peterborough, and then to Stoddard. Back then—and "back then" was 1768—back then Stoddard was truly the wilderness. The closest neighbors were in Peterborough or Keene or Walpole. There were no roads, only paths through the dense forest.

But John Taggert and his wife cleared the land and built a house and began farming. It was, as you can imagine, a hard life.

In the late 1700s, there was an especially hard winter and by mid-February the Taggert family had run out of food.

A blizzard had snowed the family in. But John Taggert girded himself against the elements and went off into the blowing snow toward Peterborough. There he would get food for the family.

As he trudged through the forest it again began to snow, a howling blizzard, and John almost did not make it to Peterborough. Even when he arrived and was given flour and bacon and corn, he could not move. The blowing snow was too much.

It was, in fact, nine days before he could depart Peterborough. Hand-pulling a sled, the trip to Stoddard was another two days. It had snowed another three feet atop the snow that was already there.

When he arrived at his house in the woods it was evening. John Taggert saw his home from afar and was paralyzed. Had the family survived? The thought was too much to ponder and he could hardly bring himself to go the final quarter mile.

Even at the door he paused until he heard voices. Gingerly he opened the door and he said, "Be ye all alive?"

The answer was, yes! Hungry . . . starving, in fact, but alive. And amid hugs and tears there was nothing but joy in that house.

## Snow in July

ROBERT THOMAS PUBLISHED the first *Old Farmer's Almanac* in 1792. At the time, almanacs were the most popular and most-read publications in the country. As a result, more than a dozen of these publications were vying with each other for readership.

But Robert Thomas' *Old Farmer's Almanac* had something that year that none of the others had. Seems someone at the printing shop was asleep at the press or had it in for Robert Thomas. Whatever the reason, that issue went to press with a gigantic mistake in the weather forecast. Some idiot put that there would be "snow in July" in 1792.

Publisher Thomas was sure that this would be his first . . . and his last almanac.

Well, you guessed it; it snowed in July in 1792. And word got around. Robert Thomas' *Old Farmer's Almanac* had done something amazing. And from that time on *The Old Farmer's Almanac* has continued to be the best-selling almanac in America.

*The Old Farmer's Almanac* is, of course, published nowadays in Dublin. And nowadays they use computers and other high-tech equipment to predict the weather, but they have never again been as accurate as they were in their first edition more than two hundred years ago.

# Richard Waldron

*This bronze tribute to Richard Waldron can be found in Dover.*

IN THE VERY early days, Dover consisted of a dozen or so garrison houses.

This place was then called "Cocheco" after the river and falls that ran through the town.

The falls provided drinking water and power to run a sawmill. In the seventeenth century, fishing and fur trading and supplying masts for the British navy were the main occupations. The fishing and mast-tree harvesting was done by the European settlers who were licensed by the Crown in England through the General Court in Boston. The fur trade was also licensed, but most of the furs were obtained by trade with the Native Americans of the area. New Hampshire, by the way, was a part of Massachusetts back then.

In the 1600s, the most powerful man in what is now Dover was Richard Waldron. Waldron controlled all the commerce in the Cocheco area. Anyone doing business on the Seacoast paid money to Richard Waldron. He was feared because he was rich and a major in the militia. He had soldiers to back up his decisions.

In 1676, there had been fighting between the settlers and the Native Americans in Massachusetts.

Some 400 had shown up in the area around the Cocheco settlement. Waldron saw a chance to eliminate some enemies. What he did was invite all the visiting Native Americans to a sham battle. There would be dancing and games and free food. Lots of fun.

A couple hundred Native Americans showed up for the festivities and, at one point, two companies of Massachusetts soldiers appeared on the edges of the field and put them under chains and on a ship bound for Boston.

From there the Native Americans were taken to the West Indies to be sold as slaves. No one, however, would purchase the Indians because they made terrible slaves. They would die before responding to the lash. As a result, the entire 200 natives were unloaded onto a small island where they were left to starve.

Sixteen years went by. In 1689, William and Mary replaced King James II on the English throne. James had fled to France, and there was war between the two countries. The French knew the English got their masts from the forests around Cocheco and they began supplying the Abenaki and the Pennacooks with firearms. The Native Americans met at what is now Concord and planned an attack on Cocheco.

Word of the attack was sent to Boston, and a messenger was dispatched to warn Major Waldron and the settlers there.

On June 28 of that year, some of the women of the tribes appeared at the different garrison houses in Cocheco to ask if they might sleep near the fires inside. This was common practice in colonial New Hampshire, and the women were allowed in. Just before dawn the women opened the locked doors to the braves ... and a bloody massacre took place. Before it was over most of the houses were burned. Twenty-nine people were taken captive and twenty-three others were killed, many tortured to death.

Major Waldron himself was an old man by this time. He was seventy-four. He was tied to his chair in his kitchen and his shirt was cut off. A dozen Native Americans lined up to cut an "X" on his chest and, as each brave deepened the cut, he said, "This cancels your debt to me."

Finally one of them held the major's sword on the floor with the point in the air and Major Waldron was allowed to fall on it, and his pain was over.

The messenger from Boston, by the way, was stuck on the south side of the Merrimack River where he could not get a boat because of choppy water.

The day was bloody and horrible. But it was a day that went down in history. For that is where the first battle of the French and Indian Wars happened. The spot is as important in American history as Lexington and Concord, or Pearl Harbor, or Fort Sumter. Because that is where it all started.

# Frances Deering Wentworth

HER NAME WAS Frances Deering Wentworth. She was the beautiful and accomplished daughter of Samuel Wentworth of Boston.

Sometime around 1753 she fell in love with her cousin, John Wentworth of Portsmouth. At the time, John was a student at Harvard College. But after his graduation from Harvard in 1755, John's family sent him to England to finish his education and to make political connections that were so important in that day to persons of his class. He did not know when he would return.

In the meantime, another cousin of Miss Wentworth, one Theodore Atkinson Jr., also of Portsmouth, became smitten with the young lady and asked for her hand. Theodore was an only child and all his life he was to suffer from ill health.

After the couple married, they moved in with the groom's parents in their house on Court Street in Portsmouth. Then, after five years of marriage, John Wentworth returned to Portsmouth "clothed with the regalia of Governor of New Hampshire." To make matters worse, the governor's mansion on Pleasant Street was within sight of the Atkinson home.

Right off, the new governor visited the couple to pay his respects and was, from that time on, a frequent visitor to the home. The wags of the time said that there were certain signals from the upstairs rooms of the two houses. But that, of course, was only rumor.

But then, on Saturday, October 28, 1769, poor Teddy Atkinson fell sick and died in his bed. He was only thirty-three.

Governor Wentworth ordered an official day of mourning. As the body was carried from the old house to its final resting place in a tomb at St. John's Episcopal Church Graveyard, a salute of guns was fired from the fort at Newcastle and answered with a salute of gunfire from the ship-of-war Beaver, anchored in Portsmouth harbor.

The widow, all in black, followed her husband's body to the graveyard.

The next day was Sunday, and the widow again appeared in her black clothes with veil and hat.

But, it turned out, this would be the only Sunday the widow would wear black. Just ten days after the funeral, there was another procession from the old house to the same church. This time it was coach and four, and an elegant groom and a blooming widow.

The minister, the venerable and most Reverend Arthur Brown, who had just intoned, "Ashes to ashes and dust to dust," was now intoning, "For better or for worse!" The poor man was beside himself with confusion.

*The Boston Newsletter* of November 17, 1769, carried the announcement. It read:

> This morning his Excellency John Wentworth, Esq., our worthy and beloved Governor, was married by the Reverend Mr. Brown to Mrs. Frances Atkinson, widow of the honorable Theodore Atkinson, Jr. Esq., deceased.

It went on:

> The bride was adorned with every accomplishment requisite to make the marriage state agreeable.

What the article failed to mention was that the minister, the Reverend Arthur Brown, in his shocked and flustered state, tripped as he left the church after the ceremony, and broke his arm.

# Martha's Second Wentworth

THE WENTWORTH COOLIDGE mansion on Little Harbor in Portsmouth has been the witness to many scandals.

It was there that the Royal Governor Benning Wentworth married the scullery maid, Martha Hilton, when he was sixty and she only twenty years old. The marriage had tongues wagging all over New England. It was a juicy piece of gossip. Still is.

The marriage came after the governor's wife and three sons had all died. He had no heirs then . . . and was a widower. Martha shared his bed for the next dozen years and, for her fidelity at his death in 1770, she was given this grand mansion and a considerable fortune. She also had the title "Lady Wentworth."

It would be nice to say that after the governor's death, Lady Wentworth was inconsolable. But that was not the case. In fact, Lady Wentworth was very consolable. And the man who consoled her was a retired British Army officer, one Colonel Michael Wentworth, a distant relative to the deceased Benning Wentworth.

Colonel Wentworth had all the faults that the governor had had, and more. He was arrogant and imperious and dishonest and a bounder. He also was an inveterate gambler.

But he was something the governor had never been, he was handsome and dashing. He was also a fine horseman. He once made a trip from Boston to Portsmouth in less than one day, leaving that morning and arriving at eight that evening.

Martha was smitten. And so they were married. They had one child, a daughter whom they named after her mother, Martha.

When President George Washington came to Portsmouth in 1789, one of the first places he came to visit was the mansion. The president arrived by boat. There he enjoyed a repast and played some games and heard a recital on the harpsichord played by the colonel himself.

The Wentworths then accompanied the president back to Portsmouth by land. But the high living caught up with Colonel Wentworth. He gambled away his own fortune and then most of his wife's. He died in New York City. Historian Charles Brewster says it may have been a suicide. Martha outlived him by many years and lived modestly but comfortably.

Their daughter married another Wentworth, one Sir John Wentworth, an Englishman who practiced law in Portsmouth. They lived in the house until 1816. She died in London in 1851.

Colonel Wentworth's last words before he killed himself are supposed to have been, "I have had my cake . . . and ate it."

# William Whipple's Wedding

WILLIAM WHIPPLE, AS you probably know, is one of two New Hampshire men to sign the Declaration of Independence. The other was, of course, Matthew Thornton.

We tend to give such men heroic status. But, as the saying goes, no man is a hero to his own valet. That is to say, there is usually some evil as well as good in any person's character.

And so it was with Billy Whipple. Yeah, he put it on the line when it came to facing England, and that took courage. Had England won he probably would have been hanged.

But Whipple was also a rich man. He had a lot to gain if England and her taxes were out of the picture. He was also a gambler and liked taking chances.

And William Whipple was also, it seems, cruel and crass. He commanded his own ship before he was twenty. The vessel was a slave ship plying the sea between Africa and the West Indies. There was tremendous money to be made slaving, and William Whipple made a lot of money.

With his nest egg, he returned to Portsmouth and continued in the mercantile business. He purchased a large home on Market Square and became part of the city's social community.

Soon he had his eye on the prettiest woman in town, his cousin, Miss Mehitable Odiorne; and, yes, this is the family for which Odiorne Point is named. He asked Miss Mehitable for her hand and was accepted.

The ceremony was to take place in the groom's home after dark. There were dozens of candles in all the rooms. The fireplace was festooned with fresh spruce. Flowers ornamented the mantle. The floors were bleached and sanded for dancing. Whipple's two black slaves, Cuffee and Prince, dressed in livery, stood at the groaning table overflowing with imported foods.

The entire social community was there.

The Reverend Samuel Langdon, wearing his flowing wig, entered the house to perform the ceremony.

All was ready. The parents and siblings of the bride along with the bridesmaids stood at one side, the groom and his attendants at the other. Suddenly the bride ran from the room.

A half-hour passed. An attendant appeared with a note. The groom went to another room to find the bride out of her gown and wearing her common dress. "I cannot go through with it," she said, "perhaps some other time."

"We must be married now or never," he said.

"Then never," she said.

And the bridegroom left the room, never again to speak to his once-betrothed.

William Whipple later married another cousin, Catherine Moffatt. They had one child who died in infancy.

And, by the way, Mehitable was later to marry William Treadwell, another rich man.

# Leonard Wood

I DON'T KNOW if you know this, but the man who was Teddy Roosevelt's commander when the Rough Riders charged up San Juan Hill in the Spanish American War came from Winchester. Roosevelt was second in command. This guy, in fact, ran the show.

This same guy, like Teddy Roosevelt, also ran for president of the United States. He was White House physician to Grover Cleveland. He was Army chief of staff under Taft.

He also won a Medal of Honor and was the guy who finally captured Geronimo in the Indian Wars in Mexico.

There is even a U.S. Army Fort in Missouri that bears his name. Now there's a hint, I bet you got it by now. Right, the guy we are talking about is Major General Leonard Wood.

And his hometown is Winchester, New Hampshire.

OK, maybe you don't know the name Leonard Wood. Not a lot has been written about him of late . . . but he was some guy.

Like I say, he was born in Winchester. His dad was a physician, Dr. Charles Wood, who served in the Civil War and contracted malaria.

After the war the family moved to the seashore.

Because his dad was a war hero, young Leonard wanted to get into West Point or Annapolis. He passed the tests but his family didn't have the political clout.

So Leonard went to Harvard Medical School. Graduated in 1884.

But then he was fired from his first job at Boston City Hospital because he wouldn't take orders and couldn't suffer fools. He was way too opinionated.

Then he heard about a position in the U.S. Army Medical Corps that was up for a competition. Dozens of doctors applied. The test was a killer, but Leonard Wood got the highest score and the job.

They sent him to Arizona Territory to put down the Apache guerrilla war. He served two years and accompanied General Miles and Captain Lawton in their pursuit of Geronimo.

The army rode three thousand miles in this mission. Doctor Wood was bitten by a tarantula and had to keep the wound open with a scalpel and bleeding constantly to rid him of the poison. He was in terrible pain.

And because he never once complained but did his job as well, he was recommended for the Medal of Honor . . . which he received.

Other Army officers, especially West Point men, were livid that this "Johnny come lately" had received such an honor.

Back home in Washington, D.C., he married well . . . a socialite . . . Louisa Condit Smith, who saw that he met important people. One of them was Teddy Roosevelt.

At the outbreak of the Spanish American War, the two men created the "First Volunteer Cavalry." And that led to San Juan Hill.

In one year, Doctor Wood was promoted from captain to brigadier general and then to major general. The regular Army Officer Corps was angry. Doctor Wood now had some very dangerous enemies.

He was then sent to be military governor in Cuba. It was Doctor Wood who hired and gave full discretionary power to Major Walter Reed to do experiments on men with the goal of eradicating yellow fever.

The result was the total eradication of the disease from Cuba.

In 1910 he was made chief of staff of the U.S. Army.

There is so much about this man that we have to skip much of it.

But you can imagine there were lots of officers and politicians out to get him. He made an enemy of President Wilson by calling him a fool for waiting too long to get into the First World War. The result was that Wilson chose General John Pershing over Doctor Wood to head the U.S. forces in that war.

In the 1920 Republican Convention, General Leonard Wood tossed his hat in the ring but lost to Warren Harding.

His final assignment was as governor general in the Philippines.

He returned home in 1927 and went into Brigham Hospital in Boston for an operation for a brain tumor. He died on the operating table.

In December of 1940, a year before Pearl Harbor, ground was broken for one of the largest military reservations in America, 71,000 acres. In a modest ceremony the place was christened "Fort Leonard Wood."

Pretty neat for a guy born in Winchester, New Hampshire.

# THE WETHERBEES

## Aunt Ethel Goosed

ETHEL PUTNAM WAS as classy and as nice a person as I ever met. Back in the early fifties, she would often stop at my parents' home for lunch. She was always welcome.

We called her "Aunt Ethel," and even then, she wasn't young. She was, in fact, over eighty and still drove a car (a 1937 Chevy) and hiked and swam. Although, since her heart attack, she only swam sidestroke. Nonetheless, in the summer she would swim the entire length of Silver Lake in Hollis . . . and back.

So on this day, Aunt Ethel had come for lunch and we kids—I had three younger brothers and a sister—we kids were running from the living room to the dining room for lunch. We had to eat fast, 'cause we had to get back to school.

Aunt Ethel was about to use the phone in the living room and was bending over to pick up the telephone directory from the floor. We kids bounded by and my brother Robbie was just in front of me and as he passed Aunt Ethel, he reached out and goosed her.

Well, the sweet old lady straightened up and spun around to look me straight in the eye.

"I. Um. Oh. No. MMMMneh." I said, and ran to the table where everyone was giggling.

Aunt Ethel came in and sat and regarded me across the table.

Robbie was looking like an angel.

Brother Charlie was laughing so hard, in fact, that Father said, "Charles, you are excused." And Charlie left the table.

"Margaret, you are excused," Father said. And my sister left the table.

Then it was, "Carl, you are excused," and, "Fritz, you are excused."

Mother came out to the kitchen. "What happened?"

We told her.

She went back to the dining room. Now only Father and Mother and Aunt Ethel were left at the table. Mother took one look at Aunt Ethel and put soup through her nose. And my father himself stormed off. And Aunt Ethel finished her meal alone.

# The Milkman

IT WAS THE middle of January 1950.

Back then Mark Wheeler had a milk delivery business in Milford and in Peterborough.

You may not remember milk delivery, but back then most people didn't buy milk at the market (notice I didn't say "supermarket"... because most towns didn't have supermarkets then). Most people back then had their milk delivered. Milk came in glass bottles, and there wasn't much homogenized milk. Back then the cream was floating on the top in the narrow part of the bottle.

You left your empty bottles on your front step with a note in the top telling the milkman how many bottles to leave.

In Manchester, when I was growing up, the milkman came in a cart pulled by a horse and the horse knew which houses to stop at.

In Milford the milkmen were Frank Cassarino, and the Norwoods and the Wheelers.

Mark Wheeler's son Eddie was a basketball player in junior high. Bill McGee was on the team . . . Dougie Claire.

Because Mark's business was in Milford and in Peterborough, he had set up a basketball game pitting the Milford kids against the Peterborough kids. The game was on a Sunday and Mark loaded the Milford kids into one of his milk trucks and took them to the gym in Peterborough where they played the game.

Back then no one thought anything about such an arrangement. Nowadays they'd insist on special insurance and all sorts of bureaucratic stuff. But not then.

Well, after the game, the kids got back in the milk truck, and Mark started for home. But on the west side of Wilton the truck broke down. It was dusk and Mark waited for some good Samaritan to stop. But none did.

That is, until suddenly a couple cruisers pulled up and the cops, with their hands over their revolvers, approached the vehicle and ordered everyone out. Mark and the kids were, to put it mildly, shocked. What had they done? Well, they got out of the truck, and the cops got a bit of a laugh.

Here's the story:

Seems this was the day of the big Brinks robbery in Boston. Robbers had gotten away with better than a million dollars and everyone was on the lookout for a truck that had been reported parked near the scene.

Someone passed by and thought that Mark Wheeler's milk truck might just be the wanted vehicle.

The cops called a garage, and the kids were home in an hour or so. With a heck of a story to tell their parents.

# My First Horse Race

ROCKINGHAM PARK RACE track turned one hundred in 2006. I was around for half of its history.

And, in fact, I owe my first bet on a horserace to a deceased undertaker.

Leon Tucker had the Tucker Funeral Home across the street from the house my family lived in in Milford back in the 1940s. The Tuckers, Leon and Nina, were family friends.

He was a charming guy and as nice as anyone I ever knew. But he died.

Now, Nina asked my mother if I might like to have any of Leon's clothes and Mother said, of course. And so it was that I, at the age of fifteen, inherited a very expensive seersucker summer suit.

Back then (and "back then" was 1951), there were tailors in most towns who would "take in" or "let out" a garment. And I got my first suit of clothes ever. Of course, I also looked like a funeral director in it.

Well, that summer I was working as a house painter with my Uncle Ned. Uncle Ned was a dandy and a sporting guy, and he went to the track a lot. When he saw me in Leon Tucker's suit, he decided he could easily get me into Rockingham Park for my first horserace.

And so, on a Saturday, we drove over to Salem, and nobody asked any questions. I got right in.

Now, I have to say that at fifteen years old I looked twelve. I have no idea how I passed for twenty-one. I guess everyone just looked at the suit.

But what a day it was. I, in fact, won. I had ten dollars and bet the two-dollar window all day and went home with twenty-some dollars.

Uncle Ned lost that day and never took me to the track again. I guess he thought the suit was a jinx.

# The Country Club

IT WAS THE fall of 1959, and I was in the Army, stationed with the Third Cavalry at Fort Meade, Maryland.

Down at the service club on base there was a sign-up sheet on the bulletin board saying that they were putting together a show and were looking for singers and comedians and jugglers and the like to go to a mental institution outside of Baltimore and entertain the patients there.

There was a band, and there were some people who had signed up that I knew. I had never had a chance to sing with a band, and I thought this was a great opportunity so I signed up.

Later on that week the sergeant who ran the service club took me aside and told me that the asylum they were playing was an African-American facility, and I was the only white person who had volunteered. Did I want to reconsider?

Well, in 1959, there was strict segregation in the South. Every restaurant south of Delaware had a sign that said, "We reserve the right to refuse service to any one." The fact was, there were no integrated restaurants in Maryland. If a black guy had a date, he had to get food from a window and eat in the car.

Washington, D.C. was integrated but the rest of the South was the same as it was in 1870. And, as you see, even the mental institutions were segregated.

So I had a choice.

"Can I go?" I asked the sergeant.

"I guess so," he said.

"Yeah," I said, "Sounds like an adventure."

Well, it was an adventure.

The night of the show, I got on a bus in front of the service club with a couple dozen African American GIs and we rode to Crownsville. There was a huge hall with a big stage, such as you might find in a large city high school.

The show went off and the audience was tough. A bunch of black faces with mental problems is not the easiest room to work.

I sang (I remember), "A Foggy Day in London Town." I guess I wasn't very good because people in the audience told me so. But I bulled it through and, frankly, gave up singing forever.

And then the show was over.

As I was going back to the bus, one of the guys I knew, a GI named Vernon McCrae, invited me to ride back to the fort with a bunch of his friends, most of whom I also knew. So I squeezed into an old rusting pink and gray Buick with about seven other men.

There was a bottle of sweet wine, and it was passed around and the car went lumbering back toward Laurel, Maryland, with everyone singing doo-wop and drinking wine.

Then someone said, "Let's go to the Country Club."

"Hey, we got Wetherbee," someone else said.

"He's OK," someone else said.

"I dunno," someone else said.

And so we drove down this old dirt road and then took a left onto an even narrower dirt road for a couple miles and then another left up a very long driveway. In the distance in the moonlight I saw an old southern farmhouse with a dilapidated porch. We drove around back and parked and walked up and around and onto the porch and into a hallway.

To the left there was a room full of junk and a juke box playing very loud. The hallway went straight back and down a couple steps where there was a bar with pickled eggs and pickled pigs' feet. They served fried chicken and beer. To the left of the hall was another room with a second room behind it. The wall had been torn out between the two rooms making one big room. In that room were tables and chairs and tablecloths and candles on the tables and at the tables with their dates. I saw every black officer I knew at Fort Meade.

I walked into the room and conversation ceased. Every eye in the place was on me. Then Vernon McCrea came up behind me and hit me on the shoulder and with the rest of the guys swooped me out of the room and down the hall toward the bar.

I had a beer and some chicken. And after half an hour or so we all left and went back to the squad bay to sleep.

And that's the story.

That was forty-eight years ago. A lot has happened to me since then. But, you know, I can't think of another thing that has happened in my life that has made me feel as honored as I felt that night.

# Fritz the Beatnik

I USED TO be a Beatnik. I mean, I was a serious Beatnik.

I, frankly, am too old to have been a Hippie. I tried being a Hippie when it was in vogue, but no one was fooled. People used to say, "Who's that Beatnik hanging around with those Hippies?"

I played the bongos and had a beard and wore black turtleneck shirts and black trousers and sandals. In 1957 I read Jack Kerouac's *On the Road*. I identified.

In 1960, I got out of the U.S. Army and, a month or so later, moved to New York City, where I wrote poetry and read it in the coffeehouses in Greenwich Village.

I was a regular at a place called Charley Washburn's "Third Side Café" on West Third Street. An old Army buddy named Tom Pinch played guitar while I recited.

On the bill at the "Third Side Café" was an African American woman who lifted weights and sang integration songs. She called herself "Barbell Millie," and you didn't mess with her.

Another old Army buddy also was a regular at the cafe. Luke Faust was a five-string banjo player who did traditional stuff no one could stand. Luke had been kicked out of the Army because they found out that his mother was a card-carrying Communist. Luke looked like Orville Redenbacher; but still, he was not a Communist, just a banjo player.

My accompanist, Tom Pinch, was one of the first Scientologists in America. He knew L. Ron Hubbard personally. I saw Tom a few years ago. He came to New Hampshire for a visit. He is no longer a Scientologist, and he is married to a woman who looks like Imogene Coco. It was for his wife that he changed his name. He is now Tom Franklin, and he writes books with titles like *How Never to Forget Anything*. I think that's the title.

Bob Dylan used to come into Charley Washburn's "Third Side Café" late at night, after the clubs closed. See in 1960–61 the clubs had to close at midnight in New York City.

Dylan always had a big entourage with him, and I used to cut out when he arrived. He was just a kid then and I, frankly, didn't see the talent he had. I don't think he'd remember me.

One night a guy named Larry Love came in with his agent and a couple cheap women who stood in the back and applauded when he did his act. No one in the audience applauded though. Larry sang "The Good Ship Lollypop" and accompanied himself on the ukulele. A few years later, when I had a family and was living in Jaffrey, I saw him on *Laugh In*. He had changed his name to "Tiny Tim."

One of these days I'll do the act for you that I did in the coffeehouses. If you are interested.

# Happy Birthday, Paul

PAUL MCCARTNEY IS 65!

My gosh, but it is hard to believe.

I was twenty-eight years old when they arrived for the *Ed Sullivan Show* back in 1964. I frankly was too old to think much about them at that time. I had a family and a job to hold. But the radio was filled with Beatles, and the television had stories about them all the time.

Much of the to-do about them was due to their haircuts. It wasn't long before a lot of young men were sporting "Beatle Cuts" much to the disgust of their parents.

The older kids held out the longest. The crew cut was still the most popular hairstyle. That was the cut for the kids right after Word War II and right into the time of the Korean War. Our heroes then were GIs. But the Beatles changed all that.

But even as late as 1968, I remember my sister and her boyfriend going to a costume dance at UNH dressed as "hippies." It was all a laugh.

Little did they know that within three years my sister would be on her way across the country in an old school bus with a wood stove in it for heat. The "Hippie" outfit she wore everyday then was not a costume for a dance.

The Vietnam War tore the country down the middle. The young men who supported it had short haircuts, and those who marched against it had long haircuts.

You heard it every day on the street . . . someone rolling down their window to yell at some kid, "Get a haircut."

I ran across an item from Nathaniel Adams' history, *The Annals of Portsmouth*, about laws in New Hampshire in the seventeenth century. In 1639 the Colonial general court passed a law stating this:

> For as much as the wearing of long hair, after the manner of ruffians and barbarous Indians, has begun to invade New England, contrary to the rule of God's word, which says it is a shame for men to wear long hair. . . . We the magistrates who have subscribed this paper . . . do declare and manifest our dislike and detestation against the wearing of such long

hair . . . whereby men do deform themselves and offend sober and modest men, and do corrupt good manners.

And so it was 'til the American Revolution when, by then, most men pulled their hair back in a ponytail or wore it a la Benjamin Franklin who, had he been alive 200 years later, would have probably loved The Beatles.

Oh, Happy Birthday, Paul.

# The Candidates

IN THE YEARS I have lived in the Granite State, I have seen a lot of primaries.

My first experience was in 1956 when Estes Kefauver came to my hometown of Milford.

I was a photography nut, and I went down to the old Oval Restaurant and snapped a photo of the guy as he came in the door.

One of his aides gave me an address to send the photo to, and I got five bucks for it, which was a lot of money back then.

Kefauver got the vice president spot on the ticket, running with Adlai Stevenson that year. I often wondered if my photo had anything to do with his losing. Not that it mattered, my family was Republican. My dad had campaigned for Wendell Wilkie against Franklin Roosevelt. We had hundreds of Willkie buttons around the house.

That was odd, as my dad worked, as it were, for Roosevelt. See, during the Depression, Dad was the director of a National Youth Administration camp up in Lincoln. The NYA was one of Roosevelt's Works Progress Administration programs. Later in his old age, Dad voted for Arnie Arnesen for governor of New Hampshire.

Winston Churchill said that he didn't trust anyone who was not a liberal in their youth (because it showed they had no heart) . . . or a conservative in their old age (for it showed, he said, they had no brain).

I'm not sure what this says about my dad.

I shook Richard Nixon's hand once in Hillsboro. He was shooting a commercial there. I was shocked at the amount of makeup he had on. He looked like Mel Brooks as Louis XIV. All that was missing was the little mole above his lip. I thought then that he was compensating for not wearing makeup in the Kennedy-Nixon debates earlier.

Mother always said, "Take off your makeup before you go to bed." Good advice.

I've got a photograph somewhere of me with Barry Goldwater. I was not a supporter, but Wayne Green said he'd take me down to see Goldwater in his Porsche, and I wanted the ride. Wayne drove like a madman and I was sure we were going to die on the way. I never rode with him again. Goldwater turned out to be neat, and later I wished I'd voted for him.

I saw Dwight Eisenhower once from afar. I was in the Army and roaming around Washington, D.C. one afternoon. That week, Charles DeGaulle had come visiting. There in front of Blair House the two great men posed for photographs and waved at the crowd. I was thrilled.

That, of course, was not in New Hampshire.

Just by staying here in New Hampshire I have met Margaret Chase Smith, Nelson Rockefeller, Harold Stassen, Ronald Reagan, Hubert Humphrey, Sam Yorty, Ralph Nader . . . hundreds of names well known and forgotten.

There is an old joke about New Hampshire. A newsperson asks a Granite Stater if he's going to vote for a certain candidate, and the Yankee answers that he doesn't know, "I only met him twice," he says.

That is so true, it's almost not funny.

# Harold Stassen

THE NEW HAMPSHIRE Primary always attracts a lot of candidates who don't have a snowball's chance of winning.

It only costs a thousand dollars to get on the ballot and that means that anyone can get some attention every four years. The press is always looking for some different story . . . some oddity.

And so, with those who have a chance at the Oval Office come those who enter the primary for different reasons. Some just want attention. Some want to call attention to their cause.

The Green Party and Ralph Nader come to mind, as do the Libertarians and Lyndon LaRouche.

For some time, comedian Pat Paulsen entered the primary every four years to get some attention to his act. I filmed Pat Paulsen up at the now defunct Belknap College in Center Harbor back in the Seventies. I didn't think he was very funny.

Al Sharpton and Dennis Kucinich know theirs is a lost cause.

But the lost cause of all lost causes was probably Harold Stassen.

I interviewed him back in 1964, when I was a reporter with the *Monadnock Ledger*.

Harold Stassen was quite a man. He was the youngest governor ever in the history of Minnesota. Thirty-one years old. Re-elected twice. Gave the keynote address at the 1940 Republican Convention. He was a war hero and an aide to Admiral Bull Halsey in the South Pacific. Later he was the president of the University of Pennsylvania. And he helped found the United Nations.

After the war, Harold Stassen almost became the Republican presidential nominee. He lost by only a few votes to Thomas Dewey.

It was heady stuff and Harold Stassen was hooked. He was, in effect, a political addict and nine times he ran again and again for the nomination. And each time he received fewer and fewer votes. It should have been humiliating, but he didn't seem to realize it.

He was also inept as a public speaker. He once told a crowd who had come to see him in Laconia that it was a thrill for him to be back in Lebanon.

That day in Jaffrey, I remember he stood in the rain with a public address system on the back of a trailer and gave a fifteen minute speech to a crowd which consisted simply of Jaffrey Police Chief Arthur Rivard and his dog.

The rest of us were over in Pauline's Coffee Shoppe getting warm and looking out the window with people asking, "Who's that damn fool?"

Stassen then came over to the coffee shop and shook everyone's hand. I asked him a few questions and he left.

His last New Hampshire Primary hurrah was about fifteen years ago. I saw him then and didn't recognize him. He had taken to wearing a wig. It didn't quite fit. Looked to me like desperation.

Harold Stassen, by the way, died in March of 2001. He was 93 years old.

# Tickie Dickie

IF YOU ARE old enough to remember when Richard Nixon was president, no doubt you are old enough to remember the soubriquet he was given.

Some people (usually Democrats) called him "Tricky Dick."

Later, the Republicans were to get their revenge by calling President Bill Clinton "Slick Willie." In some ways it was the same nickname.

But about 1970 some enterprising company put out a wristwatch with President Richard Nixon's picture on the dial. They called the watch, "The Tickie Dickie."

Well, I got word that a shop in Nashua had received a shipment of "Tickie Dickies," and so I drove down and discovered that they had sold out almost immediately. There were no "Tickie Dickies" left.

However, the proprietor of the shop told me they did have a number of Spiro T. Agnew watches left. Well, I'd come all the way down to Nashua . . . so I bought the Spiro T. Agnew watch.

Now, if you don't remember Spiro T. Agnew, let me refresh your memory.

Agnew was vice president under Nixon and he, Agnew, was a pit bull when it came to defending the administration. This was during Vietnam and Spiro T. Agnew was the one who went on the attack against the liberals and radicals and anti-war people.

Who can forget his "nattering nabobs of negativism"? The speech that came from, incidentally, was not written by Agnew but by speech writer William Safire.

Problem was, of course, Spiro T. Agnew was also a crook. Agnew was on the take. He had accepted construction kickbacks when he had been governor of Maryland. The FBI had the goods on him, and he was forced to resign. He ended out his years as a house guest of Frank Sinatra.

My Spiro T. Agnew watch suffered no better . . . it stopped ticking in three days.

I bet if I'd gotten a "Tickie Dickie" it would still be ticking.

# Gary Hart

I STARTED OUT as a newspaper reporter on the old *Monadnock Ledger* back in 1962. In 1969, and for the next ten years, I was a TV news cameraman. In 1976, and for the next ten years, I was a newsperson on radio stations WSCV and WSLE-FM.

Over the years, I interviewed hundreds of political candidates. If I have learned anything it is that when you interview a candidate you almost never break any news.

However, once in a while there is a candidate so ingenuous that you are amazed at what they say. Meldrim Thomson was one of those guys who didn't seem to have a filter on his conversation. He said exactly what he thought. And he was, you know, always in trouble.

Generally candidates get the same questions over and over and give the same answers over and over. Read the stories and you'll see that the *Portsmouth Herald* gets the same interview with Joe Lieberman that the *Keene Sentinel* gets.

I figured this out pretty early. As a result, I used to surprise the candidates with questions about stuff other than politics. Sometimes this would give the reader a lot more information about a candidate than they got from any canned answer or stump speech.

Case in point. I once rode from Peterborough to the Keene Airport in the back seat of a station wagon with California Senator Alan Cranston. I talked the whole way about the vegan diet he ate and why. Also in the car was a reporter from a local newspaper who was angry at me for not asking the candidate how he stood on the issues. To this day that reporter thinks I wasted the ride. But my radio listeners loved the interview.

I remember I asked Gary Hart about his haircut. I noted that his tonsure was that of a movie star, not a politician. He was so happy to be asked something different, he told me about his little-known Greek barber in Washington, D.C. He also revealed that he was about as vain as any movie star. In lots of ways the voter was more informed about the man than anything he might have said about policy and politics.

Later he was caught on the monkey business with a blonde . . . and a great haircut.

# Green Christmas

THE OLD SAYING is, "Green Christmas, full graveyards."

I guess I know what this means, but I don't know if it is true. I checked the Internet to find out where the saying came from and if it is true. They said it means more people die in a mild winter.

"Duh, I knew that." But is it true? No one knows. There have been, it appears, no blind studies. So we gotta guess. I'd say, it is not true. In fact, a green Christmas should mean fewer people in the graveyards.

Cold weather keeps people indoors breathing stale air; whereas if you can get outside your lungs should be healthier.

Also it seems to me that, if a green Christmas meant more people died, then every state south of, say Maryland, would have higher death rates. Of course, old people do go south to retire, so there may be more deaths down there for that reason.

I am harping on all this because this year we have had a green Christmas, and I have been suffering with the worst case of bronchitis I have ever had. It's killing me. I am afraid to drive past cemeteries, and I don't read the obits in the *Union Leader* for fear of finding my own name.

Did you know that in 1918 seventy people died in one week of the influenza in Manchester alone?

And I couldn't get my flu shot because the doctor said I had to be healthier. I had to lick this bronchitis first.

Jeez, I wish it would snow!

# *Adam Sandler*

IN THE YEAR 2003 . . . and the year before . . . I had the distinction of being voted the second-most popular celebrity in the state in the *New Hampshire Magazine* reader's poll.

First place both years went to comedian Adam Sandler.

Well, in 2004, *New Hampshire Magazine* finally awarded me first place. And in 2005 as well.

First place? Over Adam Sandler?

Well, the editors at *New Hampshire Magazine* told me that they decided Adam Sandler did not live in New Hampshire and thus was ineligible for the contest.

So I didn't beat him after all?!!

And what's this stuff about Mr. Sandler not being a resident of New Hampshire? Was he a resident in 2003? Was he a resident the year before?

What's going on here?

I demand a recount! (No, that doesn't make much sense, does it?)

OK, I demand a . . . well, I don't know what I demand . . . but something.

Adam Sandler!

# Thanksgiving in New Hampshire

I AM NAMED for my grandfather and that gives me a special connection with Thanksgiving.

My grandfather's name was Fred Minot Wetherbee. I was christened Fred Minot Wetherbee, the Second. I have a "II" after my name. "Fritz" is a nickname.

My grandfather was seventy-three years old when I was born in 1936. I was the first grandson. Ergo the name.

You may know that Thanksgiving was the result of a campaign by a New Hampshire-born woman, Sara Josepha Hale. She lived in Newport, and she wrote a bestseller back before the Civil War. It was called *Northwood*, and it was about the New Hampshire town of the same name. The book confronted slavery two years before *Uncle Tom's Cabin* did. Uncle Tom was also written by a New England woman . . . Stowe. She came from Maine.

Now New Hampshire's author, Sarah Hale, wrote in her novel that America ought to have an official day of thanksgiving. It was an idea she never let go of.

Later Sarah Hale became the editor of the largest women's magazine in America. The magazine was *Godey's Ladies' Book*. And every year for twenty years, Sarah Hale editorialized in her magazine that the country should have a Thanksgiving Day.

Finally, in 1863, Abraham Lincoln called Mrs. Hale in and told her that, due to her urging, he was announcing an official Thanksgiving Day to be celebrated yearly on the last Thursday in November.

So that's one of New Hampshire's connections to the holiday.

We also have another connection.

You remember from your history lessons that the Pilgrims held a day of Thanksgiving after their first year in Plymouth. They had a big meal and thanked God for his bountiful munificence that year. At their feast they had all sorts of turkey and corn and squash. But the next year, God was not so generous with the Pilgrims and, by fall, many were close to starvation.

What Governor William Bradford did was send old Miles Standish off in a boat up to what is now Ordiorne Point on the New Hampshire seacoast. See, at that time, the first settlers of New Hampshire were living there in a great house. A couple dozen men were under the leadership of a guy named David Thompson.

Thompson was a smart guy, and the men at Pannawya Plantation (which is what they called their settlement there at Ordiorne Point) were not starving. In fact, they were fishermen and had a ton of salted codfish they'd been collecting to send back to sell in jolly old England.

And David Thompson was a good guy. He, in fact, put together a care package of corn and wheat and a lot of (you guessed it) codfish, and Miles Standish sailed back to Plymouth and that's what the Pilgrims ate for their second Thanksgiving.

So New Hampshire saved the Pilgrims that year.

I think maybe here in New Hampshire we should have, not turkey, but codfish cakes to celebrate Thanksgiving. I know I'm going to include codfish cakes as a side dish on our table . . . just to remind us of the New Hampshire connection.

We should toast Sarah Josepha Hale.

Oh, I didn't tell you what the connection was between Grandfather and the holiday.

Well, it's this: Abraham Lincoln proclaimed Thanksgiving Day the very year my grandfather was born . . . so my name was, in effect, created the same year that the holiday was.

I need to toast my grandfather, too. The first Fred Minot Wetherbee.

*If you enjoyed this book, you will also enjoy:*

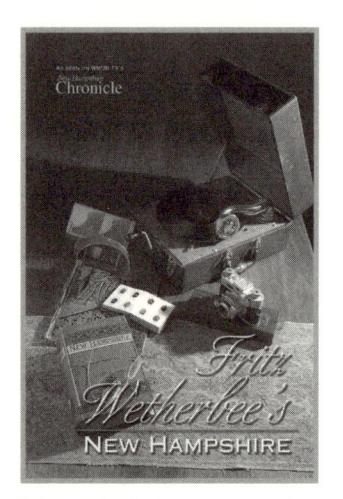

Fritz Wetherbee's New Hampshire
ISBN 978-0-9755216-5-6 / $19.95

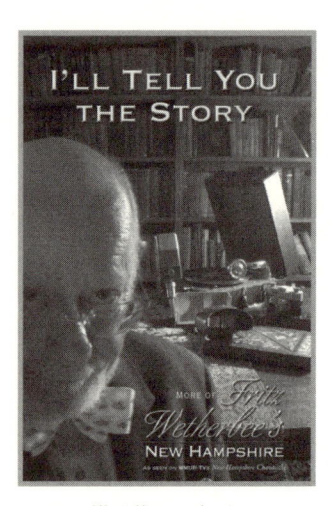

I'll Tell You the Story
ISBN 978-0-9755216-9-4 / $19.95

PLAIDSWEDE PUBLISHING
www.plaidswede.com